A TAX ON WEALTH

OTHER BOOKS BY MORTIMER LIPSKY

Quest for Peace
A Time for Hysteria
Never Again War

A TAX ON WEALTH

An Alternative to Revolution in America

Mortimer Lipsky

SOUTH BRUNSWICK AND NEW YORK:
A.S. BARNES AND COMPANY
LONDON: THOMAS YOSELOFF LTD

A.S. Barnes and Co., Inc.
Cranbury, New Jersey 08512

Thomas Yoseloff Ltd.
Magdalen House
136-148 Tooley Street
London SE1 2TT, England

Library of Congress Cataloging in Publication Data

Lipsky, Mortimer, 1915–
A tax on wealth.

Includes index.
1. Wealth tax—United States. I. Title.
HJ 4120.L55 1976 336.2'42 75-38449
ISBN 0-498-01866-0

PRINTED IN THE UNITED STATES OF AMERICA

To
GARY STEVEN

with the fervent hope that
he may, in his time, witness
social justice in America.

The people who sat in darkness have seen a great light. Our only hope today lies in our ability to recapture the revolutionary spirit and go out into a sometimes hostile world declaring eternal hostility to poverty, racism and militarism. With this powerful commitment we shall boldly challenge the status quo and unjust mores and thereby speed the day when "every valley shall be exalted, and every mountain and hill shall be made low, and the crooked shall be made straight and the rough places plain."

Martin Luther King, Jr.

Contents

Introduction

This book is addressed to the one percent of the population who owns America.

Stop and listen. Hearken to the message that is crackling loud and clear in the air of America, a message that you ignore at your peril. Hearken to the hurricane in the wind.

Georg Wilhelm Friedrich Hegel, a German philosopher, wrote a century and a half ago, "People and governments never have learned anything from history, or acted on principles deduced from it."

Does this theory, expounded so long ago, hold as true today as it did then? Will the power elite of America, like the privilégé of ancien regimes in France, Russia, China, and elsewhere, display the same narrowness of mind and short sightedness that Theodor Mommsen termed the proper and inalienable privileges of all genuine partricians?

The story is told that on 14 July 1789, when a French mob stormed the Bastille, Louis XVI wrote in his carefully kept diary just one word, "Nothing."

Martin Luther King, Jr., in his famous letter from Birmingham jail, wrote, "History is the long and tragic story of the fact that privileged groups seldom give up their august posture." Thus, French Finance Minister Colonne, in 1787, proposed that the nobility be exempt from taxation.

The question comes down to this: will the ruling class of America seize the initiative to voluntarily make the necessary changes in our society, or will it wait until these are thrust upon it by revolution?

The brutal reality is that Americans have soured on America—on its promises, its dreams, its leaders, the workings of the entire economy. Americans in every walk of life are increasingly skeptical about their political and their economic institutions. They doubt that these institutions, which are supposed to serve them, are in fact doing so. There is a growing feeling that the business community is no longer fit to govern the nation. They regard their political and business leaders not with the respect or even the tolerance of an earlier age, but with a skepticism bordering upon open hostility.

What is the basis for these grim conclusions?

Review the findings of any number of recent serious studies. A special commission established by the National Urban Coalition, headed by Mayor Lindsay of New York and Senator Fred R. Harris of Oklahoma, reported in September 1971 that, "The most disturbing point most of those we spoke with made was that they had no faith at all in the system—the government and the private wielders of power—as a protector or a provider. This disenchantment has plunged many into cynicism or apathy or despair."

According to a Louis Harris poll taken in October 1972, a majority of Americans indicated distrust of every major institution in the country—business, the press, the media, the old parties, and government in general all the way up to and including the Presidency. And this was before *Watergate* became a household word.

A survey conducted in September 1973 by the same organization for the Senate Subcommittee on Intergovernmental Relations found that a clear majority of Americans, fifty-three percent, believed that "there is something deeply wrong" in the country. Only nineteen percent showed "a great deal of confidence" in the executive branch of the Federal government; only twenty-nine percent showed a confidence in business. Five years earlier the latter percentage was fifty-nine.

In June 1972, the Opinion Research Corp. of Princeton, New Jersey found that big corporations "faced the worst attitude climate in a decade." This organization determined that, since 1965, the share of the United States public expressing low approval for business had climbed from forty-seven percent to sixty percent. This decline in approval of business was sharpest among young people. In the Harris survey only one out of every seven persons, eighteen-to-twenty-years-old, expressed confidence in the way business is run. Another survey found that forty-six percent of all Americans think big business is "dangerous to our way of life."

In March 1975, Opinion Research reported that more than half (fifty-three percent) of the population believed that "many of our largest corporations ought to be broken up."

The image of the businessman has changed from that of the bold empire builder, the heir to the heroic pioneer tradition, to that of society's plunderer.

A continuing series of studies made by the Center for Political Studies of Michigan's Institute for Social Research reported in 1964, that sixty-two percent of a nationally representative sample of adults expressed a high degree of trust in the Government. By 1970, that proportion dropped to thirty-seven percent. Among whites, those who believed that the Government was run for the benefit of all totaled 73.7 percent in 1958, 63.2 percent in 1964, 51.4 percent in 1966, 49.2 percent in 1968 and 41.3 percent in 1970. Among blacks, the corresponding percentages were 77.9 percent in 1958, 68.6 percent in 1964, 62.5 percent in 1966, 63.1 percent in 1968 and 34.1 percent in 1970.

In a little book entitled *Hopes and Fears of the American People* by Albert H. Cantril and Charles R. Roll, Jr., the authors describe the mood of America as found by two polls conducted by the Gallup organization in January and April 1971 on behalf of Potomac Associates, Inc. They discovered, "a lack of trust in most of the individuals in positions of leadership" in America. The people surveyed were gravely disturbed about the state of their country and one in four feared that the stability of the United States as a nation was now threatened. Forty-seven percent of those interviewed believed that the current unrest is likely to lead to "a real breakdown in this country."

The Roper Organization asked citizens in two hundred communities during January and February 1971: "Do you feel that things in this country are generally going in the right direction today, or do you feel that things have pretty seriously gotten off on the wrong track?" Sixty-four percent said the country was on the wrong track, twenty-three percent said right direction, and thirteen percent had no opinion. Dissatisfaction was present among every group in the country, spanning sexual, age, racial, and economic distinctions.

A survey conducted during the spring of 1971 by Daniel Yankelovich, Inc. for JDR 3d Fund found that thirty percent of college students would rather live in some other country than the United States. Seventy percent believed that such major institutions as business, political parties and the military needed drastic reform. Only thirty-nine percent thought that "hard work will always pay off."

Throughout the nation, there is a deep and pervasive feeling that things are not working. Among all segments of the population, there is a loss of faith and confidence in our society. Very few are any longer satisfied with what exists at present. We are faced with a multitude of problems that are neither comprehensible nor manageable. Right now, there is the widespread feeling that this country is not even being governed and that our leadership is impotent to do anything about it.

"America is promises", the poet once heralded. Once we feverently believed, with Thomas Jefferson, that America was the "best hope" of all mankind. Once Americans thought they were the new chosen people with a mission to lead mankind. Once we were young and eager and brave and happy and joyous and adventuresome and invincible, exultant in the excitement and possibilities of life. Once we had hope. Once the future seemed to be so pure, so radiant, so certain, so alluring in the firm conviction that our nation has progressed, is progressing, and will always and inevitably progress. Once we were caught up in a euphoria of rising expectations where the dazzling future loomed ahead as an unlimited tending upwards and onwards for all times. Once America was a dynamic scene of great ferment, bursting with exuberance, restlessness, energy, imagination, invention, and achievement; there was nothing torpid, sluggish, or slack about America in those years. Once America was the land of beauty, land of abundance, land of the free. Once it was great to be alive. Once Thomas Huxley said, "There is something sublime in the future of America."

Today, vultures circle over the American dream, now dissolved into the American nightmare. Today, the blueprints of a great society lie buried in the ruins of Watts and Detroit. Today, the can-do country has become that country that cannot. Today, the American myth is dying, the country is in disarray, in disease. Today, the sweetness has gone out of American life; no more joy, no more laughter, just constant fear.

America, at the highest point of majesty and power ever attained by any people since the fall of the Roman empire, commanding one-third of the world's wealth, is unsettled to the very roots of its being. Americans, enjoying material progress beyond the dream of kings, living in the midst of comforts undreamed of even by their own parents, are lost and adrift, bewildered, discontented, demoralized, anxious, and confused.

Abroad in America, one senses a mood of suspicion and resentment, a sense of betrayal, tones of frustration, disillusionment and alienation, disenchantment with the old politics, anger at injustice and neglect, disgust at private opulence and public squalor, indignation over fraud and bribery in government and corruption in high office, and outrage over the privileges of special interests. America has lost confidence in itself, in its destiny and in its heritage.

Americans feel in their bones that somehow they have lost their way. We have forgotten what America is all about. Our society is springing leaks everywhere; our world is giving at the seams. As de Lawd said to Noah in Marc Connelly's *Green Pastures,*" 'Everything dat's fastened down is coming loose.' The panoply of American institutions has begun to disintegrate. They just do not deliver anymore. We have simply used up the capabilities of the waxwork of our stiffly preserved nineteenth century institutions. We have lost a commanding grip on our problems.

Fifty years ago W.B. Yeats wrote a prophetic poem:

> Things fall apart; the centre cannot hold;
> Mere anarchy is loosed upon the world,
> The blood-dimmed tide is loosed, and everywhere
> The ceremony of innocence is drowned;
> The best lack all conviction, while the worst
> Are full of passionate intensity.

What happened? What went wrong? Who is to blame? What might have been? How can we explain the rising tide of violence in the streets, drug addiction, crime, the miscarriage of the social welfare systems, government corruption, a divided people, riots, revolting youth, unbreathable air, and undrinkable water?

As Alexander Hamilton expressed it two centuries ago:

> We may indeed with propriety be said to have reached almost the last stage of humiliation. What indication is there of disorder, poverty and insignificance that could befall a community so peculiarly blessed with natural advantages as we are which does not form a part of the dark catalogues of our public misfortunes?

In spite of our spectacular strides in science and technology, there is something basic that is missing. There is a pervading poverty of the spirit that stands in glaring contrast to our abundance. In the words of President Nixon, "Never has a nation seemed to have had more and enjoyed it less. . . . We have found ourselves rich in goods, but ragged in spirit."

Our abundance has brought us neither peace of mind nor serenity of spirit. There has been a colossal breakdown of optimism. The country may now be on the brink of a trauma as severe as the Civil War or the Great Depression. At all levels of American life, people suffer fears, insecurities, and gnawing doubts to such an intense degree that America may well be experiencing a kind of national nervous breakdown, a depression of the national spirit. Our ethical and moral values may have been undermined to such an extent that a state of inner terminal dry rot and disintegration has set in.

Watergate merely reflects the ugliness that has permeated every echelon of society in America. We are witnessing the ethical collapse of a civilization.

Many scholars fear that the United States as a society has begun to self-destruct. This feeling is typified by the title of Professor Andrew Hacker's book, *End of the American Era.* Professor Barrington Moore, Jr., of Harvard University writes, "In all sobriety, chaos is the direction in which American society seems to us to be heading." Professor Paul Hollander of the University of Massachusetts believes that the continuation of the American democracy can no longer be taken for granted. Professor Herbert J. Gans writes of *The American Malaise.*

We live in a deeply troubled and unsettled time. Marquis Childs stated that it was necessary to go back two thousand years to find people so filled with a foreboding sense of great and terrible impending events.

Great changes dominate the world. On every hand, old values, old standards, and old precepts are challenged; old ways uprooted. Institutions that have endured for centuries—even millennia—are being shaken and, with them, are toppling old systems of authority, status, and values. In the period of upheaval accompanying the breakup of the old order, we are witnessing the undermining of traditional norms that, over a period of many centuries, had acquired sacred connotations. All the old roots—namely, social class, marriage, property, religion, patriotism, family—are now shaking under the hurricane impact of what Alvin Toffler calls "accelerative thrust."

America now realizes, with Barry Goldwater, that it is "up to its eyebrows in trouble." America, too, now knows that it is mortal, that a civilization is as fragile as a life, that the abyss of history is deep enough to hold us all.

The American people must realize that the only people able to destroy American society are the Americans themselves. The nation faces much greater danger at home than abroad. Their interests are more in the war in the cities than it ever was in Indochina.

Arnold Toynbee has delineated how nineteen of twenty-one enumerated civilizations died from within and not by conquest from without. "Civilizations are never murdered, they die by their own hands."

A TAX ON WEALTH

1

Prerevolutionary America

A shudder of discontent is shaking America today. This deep rumbling that we hear is the thunder of disinherited masses clamoring for a fair share of the American pie.

The patterns of American history may be described as a series of pendulum swings between a dominant Hamiltonianism and a dominant Jeffersonianism. The clash between these two philosophies recurs throughout in the debates over the First and Second Banks of the United States, in struggles over free trade versus protectionism, in the bitter conflicts between the agrarian West and the industrial East, and between the agrarian South and the industrial North, in the battles between the farmers and the railroads, the corporate empire builders and the trustbusters, management and labor.

The preamble to the 1892 platform of the old Populist Party began as follows: "We meet in the midst of a nation brought to the verge of moral, political and material ruin."

Populism—or Jeffersonianism—is resurgent in America, and today a new populism is abroad in the land. It is a lineal descendant of the ancient American suspicion that the monied interests had taken over the country contrary to its democratic principles. This belief that an economic elite controls affairs by means kept hidden from the people is one that can be traced at least as far back as the political attacks of the Jeffersonians against the Hamiltonians at the end of the eighteenth century.

There is a strong tug in the national mythology that favors the rancher, the cowboy, the farmer, the worker over the banker, the railroad builder, the land speculator, the boss. The new populism speaks for the little man against the Establishment, the poor and deprived against the rich and privileged. It centers about proposals for a radical redistribution of income, wealth, and power and claims that the first priority of politics is to redress existing imbalances. Thus, public issues have been created out of private discontents.

A new generation of Tom Watsons, Cyclone Davises, Stump Ashbys, Sockless Jerry Simpsons, Mary E. Leases, and Leonidas L. Polks are stumping the country rousing people to raise "less corn and more hell." They are attempting to unite and bridge the cleavages between the discontented sections, parties, races, and classes.

No greater tragedy can befall a nation than to leave millions of people with a feeling that they have no stake in their society. Thus, America today has to make a choice: either make the basic changes in our society that will win back the loyalty of the discontented, or face the disruption and disintegration of the America we have known.

We ask with Franklin D. Roosevelt, "Will it be said that democracy was a great dream but it could not do the job?" To answer that question we have to return to the basic, underlying issue of political life: who holds power and by what right? And within these basics lies the stuff from which revolutions are fashioned.

The new populism has touched a new nerve of rage and frustration among the people and has ignited a sense of outrage that, for the first time in our history, has toppled two governments and captured a political party.

In his memorandum to the President, Daniel Moynihan stated, "In one form or another, all of the major domestic problems facing you derive from the erosion of the authority of the institutions of American society. . .All we know is that the sense of institutions being legitimate—especially the institutions of government—is the glue that holds societies together. When it weakens, things come unstuck." Well, things are unstuck now.

Lenin is said to have told a Czarist policeman on his first arrest as a student demonstrator in Kazen in December 1887, "The wall is rotten—one shove and it will collapse." With bated breath, America awaits the shove.

The Tom Watsons, Cyclone Davises, and others call in vain for help from the richly paid, the well endowed, the beneficed, the honored, the titled, the mitred, the surpliced, the coroneted aristocracy of wealth. Wendell Phillips remarked, "Revolutions are not made, they come." Thus, even if the explosive mood of the oppressed is ignored, problems still have to be solved in one way or another. In the absence of a choice to make the required basic changes in our society, the alternative is revolution.

At a conference held in October 1971 at Portland State University, Harvey Wheeler of the Center for the Study of Democratic Institutions declared that America "as presently organized" was not possible much longer and that American society was, in fact, in a prerevolutionary situation.

We have been told by our public opinion pollsters that Americans have lost hope in their future, and people who do not believe in the future are suicidal. Revolutions come out of revolting conditions: it is the language of the unheard, it is a suicidal act.

Why does the gentle reader shake his head in shocked incredulity? America is, after all, the cradle of revolution. Jean-Francois Revel states flatly that the revolution of the twentieth century will take place in the United States. He writes, "It is only there that it can happen. And it has already begun."

M. Revel sets forth five conditions that are prerequisites for revolution:

1. There must be a critique of the injustices existing in economic, social, and racial relationships.

2. There must be a critique of the management of economic affairs directed against the waste of material and human resources. This critique calls into question the goals of technological progress.

3. There must be a critique of political power and the conditions under which it is exercised, distributed, or monopolized. This critique encompasses the exclusion of the public body from participation in the decision-making processes.

4. There must be a critique of the existing tenets of culture as expressed in morality, religion, customs, philosophies, accepted beliefs, art, and literature. This critique extends to the means of distribution of that culture, that is, education, information, and communication.

5. There must be a critique of the old society as a mechanism for upholding the freedom and dignity of the individual.

These five prerequisites are present in full force in the present-day United States, and their presence has created a state of tension without which no revolution is possible.

For a society to be viable there must be a basic feeling among almost all classes of security, optimism, progress, and order; there must be an intellectual acceptance of the ideals of that society; there must be a relative absence of guilt feelings. When that national self-satisfaction, that national faith in the future is shaken by these five critiques, that society begins to topple.

The five critiques are, of course, initiated by the opinion-makers of the society and what Crane Brinton calls "the desertion of the intellectuals" is the first symptom of revolutionary unrest. The critiques, the questioning lead to that state that Max Weber termed "the decay of legitimacy."

Mr. Revel had outlined three steps towards revolution: a change in consciousness, a commitment to action, and a change in political institutions. The above five prerequisites fulfill step one. Later in this chapter we shall demonstrate that we are in the midst of step *two*.

Mr. Revel points out further that all revolutionary trends have one common factor: that a group of those who benefit from the status quo detach themselves from their class and betray it from within. This was true of a part of the French aristocracy in the eighteenth century, of a part of the Russian aristocracy in the twentieth century, and of a part of the bourgeoisie in the nineteenth and twentieth centuries. This critique from above is indispensable in the revolutionary process.

Barrington Moore, Jr. calls this process a second mutation on the road to revolution, (the decay in legitimacy being the first). It is characterized by the appearance of very sharp conflicts of interest within the dominant classes themselves.

Thus, when dissenters today are accused of being middle class—of course, they are. They could not be otherwise. This is their function in contemporary revolutionary activity: to become aware, by experience, of the internal failure of a system of life in the very milieu where it is thought to be successful; to point out, by their living examples, the failure of the system to provide the happiness it was supposed to create.

The Trojan horse in our midst that has detached itself from its class is, of course, our young people. They were the first to realize that the emperor's clothes were tawdry. The result has been, in the words of Kingman Brewster, "a sad scorn, a monumental scorn" for the political and economic processes of America.

It was Leon Trotsky who stated that, "Students are the barometer of revolution." Probably because the universities are the soft underbelly of a sick society, it was on the campuses, beginning in 1964 with Berkeley's battle over Bancroft Strip that we witnessed the revolutionary invention of our era, namely, dissent. The sit-ins, teach-ins, eat-ins, confrontations, demonstrations, marches, draft resistance, and even riots, all forms of creative disorder, are the manifestations of a new Che Guevara type of romantic insurrection. For today the real banner of unrest is the black flag of anarchy and not the red flag of Communism.

Chairman Mao's basic precept states: "It is right to rebel." We are forced to accept Jerry Rubin's verdict that the revolution has replaced the church as the country's moral authority. And Bob Dylan sings, "There's a battle outside and it's raging. It'll soon shake your windows and rattle your walls, for the times they are a changing." You do not need a weatherman to know which way the wind blows.

What is more ominous is that the young are consciously rejecting the bourgeois creed of "Work, pray, save" in favor of alternate models of future development. Many live in resistance. The scattering of communes and kids' ghettos are in this sense liberated areas.

Apologists for the old order will reply that there has always been a generation gap, that hostility between youth and age is normal. But, in the past, the criticism of youth was tinged with envy; they were impatient to replace the incumbents in order to assume in their own right the prerogatives of power. In a sense, the young were junior members of the club; their criticism had the quality of loyal opposition.

Today, rebellious youth does not identify with their elders; they show little enthusiasm for either emulating or supplanting them. They have rejected the society in which they were nurtured. They are alienated from the values held dear by their parents and contemptuous of the Establishment. The young equate the established leadership with venality, if not outright villany. America has lost her children.

As a result, our youth takes refuge in escapism. The outcome is a counter culture, a counter society, that reflects the other—worldliness and abandons the competitive system and the traditional moralities for a diversity of subcultures: experimentation in behavioral standards, sexual latitudes, outlandish dress, mind expanding drugs, sensory pleasure cults, and satisfaction in fashioning leather belts and baking organic bread instead of in turning out automobiles on an assembly line. These are symptoms of a fundamental loss of confidence in society's institutions and leadership—hence, a loss of faith in society's future.

America is thus being questioned not only by rhetoric, but also by social experimentation that is changing it from within. Here is a true laboratory of revolution. The result is a Robin Hood outlook of taking from the rich and giving to the poor.

In the latter nineteenth and early twentieth centuries we thought economic progress desirable, whatever the cost. Today we are counting the cost and finding it excessive. We are questioning the goal of economic growth—a goal that lies at the heart of capitalist development and that has shaped the form and objectives of all business. We are questioning the Protestant ethic that one's dignity depends on one's job.

We are questioning the role of the corporation itself as a social and quasi-political institution. The questioning is focusing on the contradictions between individual fulfillment and realization against business objectives of productivity and profit.

John Fowles asks what has been the "great driving obsession" of the last 150 years. He answers that, without a doubt, it was money. But he adds, "the trial of money as the unique source of happiness has begun in the richer countries of the West."

This attitude has infected industry. The young, blue collar worker, often bearded and long-haired like his campus contemporary, is rebelling against the human degradation implicit in the assembly line. The demand for a nonrepressive organization of work is finding expression in low productivity, high turnover, begrudging overtime, excessive absenteeism, individual and group sabotage, the radicalization of grievances, and in wildcat strikes such as the stoppages at the Chrysler plant in Detroit and at the highly automated General Motors Vega plant at Lordstown, Ohio.

George Gallup, Jr. told an American Management Association seminar on productivity that, in the eighteen to twenty-nine year-old age bracket, thirty-three percent of the workers consider their jobs unsatisfactory, and fully seventy percent admit that they are loafing on the job. A massive study, released in December 1972, entitled *Work in America* and prepared by the nonprofit W.E. Upjohn Institute for Employment Research for the Department of Health, Education, and Welfare, came up with results that suggested that a majority of Americans—white collar workers and blue collar workers—are discontented with their work. The report concluded that this dissatisfaction is sapping the economic and social strength of the nation. We are experiencing a great refusal.

Millions of middle class and working kids are shoplifting from the black experience, lionizing as a hero the streetman who flouts the values and laws of the mainstream. Further, the movement for social change has accompanied the youngsters from the campuses and the factories into the armed services. This gives us Barrington Moore Jr.'s third mutation: the loss of unified control over the instruments of violence, namely, the military and police.

Despite the largest expenditure of funds in peacetime history, decomposition has set in among the military forces. G.I. coffeehouses, underground newspapers, strikes, and near mutinies have cast serious doubts upon the loyalties of our armed forces. There are fears in high places that the military has been subverted. Read the article by Colonel Robert D. Heinl, Jr. entitled *The Collapse of the Armed Forces* in the 7 June 1973 issue of the *Armed Forces Journal.* Were our men returned from South Vietnam because the guns were being turned around?

Witness the court martial of Private Billy Dean Smith, later acquitted, who was accused of a fragging attack against two officers in March 1971. The Army had reported a total of 96 such incidents in 1969 and 209 in 1970, resulting in 101 deaths in two years.

The New York Times on 21 November 1970 published a letter from a soldier in Vietnam. He wrote:

> They have set up separate companies for men who have refused to go out to the field. It is no big thing here anymore to refuse to go. . . .Operations have become incredibly rag-tag; vehicles don't work for lack of maintenance; helicopters are just falling to the ground; airfields are falling apart.

This dissidence is not confined to the men in the front lines. The Army has been plagued throughout Europe by problems of drug abuse. In September 1973, General Michael S. Davison, the commander of United States Army Europe, characterized drug and alcohol abuse as the "greatest single threat to the command's readiness."

According to Barrington Moore, Jr., underground activities and racial conflicts among the troops stationed in Germany recall the behavior of the Russian soldiers prior to the collapse of 1917.

Nor has the once elite Navy been spared. Disturbances, near mutinies, and sabotage have been reported on the carriers *Saratoga, Forrestal, Kitty Hawk, Constellation* and *Ranger*, the oiler *Hassayanpa*, and other vessels.

This collapse of discipline has spread to the police forces. Witness the recurring police riots and corruption. Witness Attica. Low morale in the armed forces and the police reflects the condition of the society from which these men are recruited.

Without the control or neutralization of the instruments of violence, revolutionary movements do not have a ghost of a chance. But when the military and the police cease being dependable, when they refuse to obey the powers that be, that is revolution.

Perhaps all this is rooted in the American revolutionary spirit of 1776 whose slogan was, "Don't tread on me." For it was Thomas Jefferson who said, "The tree of liberty must be refreshed from time to time in the blood of patriots and tyrants. It is its natural manure." And it was Abraham Lincoln who echoed, "This country belongs to the people who inhabit it. Whenever they shall grow weary of the existing government, they can exercise their Constitutional right of amending it or their revolutionary right to dismember or overthrow it."

Given the probability that the required basic changes in our society will not be made voluntarily, given the possibility—perhaps, the probability—that America may be confronted with revolution, the question then is: the coming revolution, will it be pacific or violent.

Given the nature of American history, the answer is predictable. The National Commission on the Causes and Prevention of Violence found us to be a "rather bloody-minded people in both action and reaction." Arthur M. Schlesinger Jr., the historian, calls upon us to recognize "that the evil is in us, that it springs from some dark, intolerable tension in our history and our institutions." He terms the United States a land of "violent people with a violent history," and fears that "the instinct for violence" has seeped into the bloodstream of our national life. D.H. Lawrence stated that "the essential American soul is hard, isolate, stoic and a killer."

Violence has indeed been programmed into the structure of American life. Beginning with Shay's rebellion in 1786, we have suffered the anti-Irish riots of the 1840s and 1850s, the Indian massacres, the draft riots of 1863, the Ku Klux Klan and lynchings, the anti-Chinese riots of the 1870s, the Molly Maguires, the labor uprisings of the 1890s and 1930s, the anti-Negro riots of 1919 and 1960, the redneck reaction to the civil rights struggle of the 1960s, the urban riots of the late 1960s, the political assassinations, the frontier cult of the gun, organized gangsterism, My Lai, and scores of other holocausts.

The National Commission on the Causes and Prevention of Violence concluded in June 1969 that the United States, since 1948, "has been among the half-dozen most tumultuous nations in the world."

It was thus predictable that dissent would turn to resistance, and push to shove, when the dissenters realized that the power structure would respond only in a very limited way to nonviolent methods. The agitator soon realized that one had to shoot someone, burn himself alive, do something violent in order to get any attention, in order to make an impression on the absolute stonewall of indifference that confronted him. It is the hinge that squeaks that gets the grease.

Losing faith in the ballot box, the Narodniki turned to the Molotov cocktail and the streets as the only remaining means of protest. For riots and violence are the desperate language of the unheard. It has become the conviction of an increasing number of the disaffected that nothing short of revolution will prise the fingers of the unyoung, the uncolored, and the unpoor off the windpipe of our society, that concessions will be torn from the grasp of those in the seat of power only when the breaking point has been reached.

The 1968 uprising in France failed because the student leaders turned to the wrong allies. Misled by Marxist rhetoric, they had not realized that organized workers constituted the most conservative sector of society. The unionized workers, in the last two or three decades, have acquired a modicum of possessions, perhaps even a modest home. Compared to the physical degradation of the great depression, their positions have improved so much that they want to protect whatever they have and the system that has made it possible.

For the workingman, everything would be jeopardized by radical change. Once the worker has attained a position of comparative economic security with a reasonable expectation of improvement, he has considerably more reason to be conservative than the middle class executive or professional. Pork chop unionism has extinguished the revolutionary fervor of American labor.

What the French student leaders of 1968 did not grasp was that there was a class beneath the working class. This underclass lives beneath society, outside society—outcasts by whatever name you call them. Term them disaffected, under-privileged, lumpenproletariat, *descamisados* (shirtless ones), mudsills of society. They are the poor. What would have happened if the poor had joined the young on the march?

"Where the breakdown of traditional authority sets the poor of the earth on the march," writes political philosopher Hannah Arendt in *On Revolution,*

> where they left the obscurity of their misfortunes and streamed upon the market place, their furor seemed as irresistable as the motion of the stars, a torrent rushing forward with elemental force and engulfing a whole world.

President Lyndon Johnson warned, "One of the clearest lessons of modern times is the destructive power of man's oldest enemies. Where hunger, disease and ignorance abound, the conditions of violence breed." Robert S. McNamara said, "There can be no question but that there is an irrefutable relationship between violence and economic backwardness."

The largest economically backward segment of the population is, of course, comprised of the 11.3 percent of our people who are black. For over three hundred years we have overwhelmed the black with frustration, hopelessness, and despair, driven him to drink and dope, to poverty and prostitution, illiteracy and illegitimacy. What do we expect now in return: groveling servility, obsequious gratitude and fawning love—or rebellion? Sartre wrote in *Orphee Noir,*

> What then did you expect when you unbound the gag that had muted those black mouths? That they would shout your praises? Did you think that when those heads that our fathers had forcibly bowed down to the groun were raised again that you would find adoration in their eyes?

William E.B. DuBois forecast in 1900, "The problem of the twentieth century is the problem of the color-line—the relation of the darker to the lighter races of man." The Presidential Commission on Violence that was attempting to answer the question, "Where did we go wrong?" might well have studied the prophecy that concluded Dr. DuBois' 1935 work, *Black Reconstruction*, that the black's "frustration cannot indefinitely continue. Some day it may burst in fire and flood. Who will be to blame? And whose the greater cost? Black folk, after all, have little to lose, but civilization has all."

There is an ever-present danger that the black, harshly buffeted by the grim realities of poverty, hunger, danger, displacement, disease, and deprivation, beset by force and violence, will escape into paranoid visions of grandeur, into daydreams of demonic power, ecstacies of sadism, and endless fantasies with a gun, eagerly awaiting the moment when the black races will rise like the avenging Attila against the white oppressors. Witness the superman fantasies of the black movies, melodramas larded with black machismo, and constant carnage.

Thus, we do not need Rap Brown to remind us that every black is a potential traitor, every black man a potential revolutionary. Every black person belongs to the movement whether he has participated in demonstrations and riots or not. And Rap Brown speaks fact when he tells us that the brother on the street carried a knife in his diaper.

The rigidity of the political structure and the absence of hope have forced clusters of alienated blacks into social banditry where criminality has become a form of primitive social protest. Extremist rhetoric encourages many blacks, and especially the young unemployed outlaw pack, to believe that crime is a political act against a corrupt society. What whites term criminal activity, the blacks term counter attack and rebellion. Many a black enters the prison gate like a bridegroom enters the bridal chamber.

The brutal reality is that there is an adversary relationship between blacks and whites, that there is a black Trojan horse within the gates of white America. They number in excess of twenty-four million and they are full of hate. Their dreams are of Nat Turner creeping through suburbia.

The time for protest marches and singing "We Shall Overcome" has passed. The slogan now is, "Burn, baby, burn" and "Kill the pigs." The exploding ghettos and rat-ridden slums are seedbeds for revolution. The level of mass violence in the nation's cities mounts towards a level that can be described only as low-grade insurrection or guerrilla warfare.

James Baldwin predicts that "there will be bloody holding actions all over the world for years to come but the Western party is over and the white man's sun has set. Period." Given the vulnerability and the fragility of our urban technological society, a few militants can, by sabotage or a thousand other ways, gut and disrupt the entire system. Witness the disruption of Birmingham.

The pathology of the black ghettos has infected the entire country and the community that is America is rent with emmity. Hatred and venom lie close to the surface of our national life. Our society has assembled a combination of combustible materials. No one should be surprised if this tinder box ignites. To quote William Shakespeare, "So foul a sky clears not without a storm."

According to Alexandra Tolstoy, the daughter of Leo Tolstoy, the United States today is like Russia before the 1917 Revolution: "It's just the picture we had before the Revolution." Aleksandr I. Solzhenitsyn, also, compares the United States to Czarist Russia, predicting that America is "also in its final years before the great breakdown."

"The silent sullen peoples
Shall weigh your Gods and you."

2

The Disaffected

We speak glibly of the disaffected, the oppressed, the exploited, the discontented. Who are they? Alas, their number is legion. The disaffected include the poor, the hungry, the young, the aged, the blacks, the chicanos, women, farmers, the ill-housed, the sick, the Indians, the jobless, the poorly educated, the Puerto Ricans, other minorities, the Appalachians, rootless migrants, drug addicts, prisoners, blue-collar workers, commuters—in short, the nonrich and the powerless: those whom Jack London termed "the people of the abyss." Even the good American earth, poisoned by pollution, is crying for succor.

The disaffected, are they disgruntled Communists, or do they have legitimate grievances? To answer that question, we will have to explode the myth of American affluence. True, there is immense wealth in the United States but a substantial number of the people are desperately poor, unable to satisfy the primal needs of animal life, and the American society is poverty stricken. Yes, strange as it may seem, America is a grossly underdeveloped country.

In dollars we may be rich beyond the dreams of avarice, but in the things that make life worth living we are poor, and growing poorer. We suffer public squalor amid private opulence. This country plants its astronauts upon the moon while standing knee deep in garbage—Croesus on a garbage heap.

Franklin Delano Roosevelt, in his second inaugural address, best expressed the state of the nation:

> I see a United States which can demonstrate, that, under democratic methods, national wealth can be translated into a spreading volume of comfort hitherto unknown. But here is the challenge to our democracy. In this nation I see millions of its citizens and a substantial part of the whole population who at this very moment are denied the greater part of what the very lowest standards of today call the necessities of life. I see millions of families trying to live on income so meagre that the pall of family disaster hangs over them day by day. I see millions whose daily lives in city and on farms continue under conditions labeled indecent by so-called polite society one half a century ago. I see millions denied education, recreation and the opportunity to better their lot and the lot of their children. I see millions lacking the means to buy the products of farm and factory and by their poverty denying work and productiveness to many other millions. I see one-third of a nation ill-housed, ill-clad, ill-nourished. The test of our progress is not whether we add more to the abundance of those who have much; it is whether we provide enough for those who have too little.

Two score years later conditions have not changed significantly. "The poor shall never cease out of the land," says the Bible. Yes, God must have loved the poor people: he made so many of them.

Who are the poor? Benjamin Disraeli wrote,

> the rich and the poor—two nations between whom there is no intercourse and no sympathy; who are as ignorant of each others habits, thoughts, and feelings as if they were dwellers in different zones or inhabitants of different planets; who are formed by a different breeding or fed by a different food or ordered by different manners.

Richard Scammon, formerly the director of the Bureau of the Census, and Ben Wattenberg offer us a common-sense definition of poverty as that lower portion of the economic spectrum where the essentials of survival—food, clothing and shelter—cannot be taken for granted. But can this portion of the spectrum be measured numerically?

One would imagine that in this age of advanced computer technology our economists and statisticians would have pinned down a rather precise delineation of this unfortunate grouping. Far from it. Statistics of poverty are not neutral, scientific reflections of an objective fact. The given definitions fluctuate widely depending upon the axe being ground. If you are a politician in power, you tend to show progress in eliminating poverty and to understate the number of poor. If you are a politician in opposition, you tend to claim the exact reverse. Figures do not lie but liars figure. It is a great numbers game.

It is true that one cannot make blinchiki out of statistics and that such tables make dull reading and are often wrong. But if we are going to understand the concept of poverty, there must be measurement. Nor should we ever forget the crucial fact that these numbers represent people. It is necessary to grasp that poverty is a level, a gradation, a continuum. It is not a fixed point at a given time below which you are poor and above which you are wealthy. No hard and fast line separates the poor from the rest of society.

We should also be aware that the bench mark of poverty is subject to manipulation depending upon the base year used, the ingredients constituting the market basket, the effects of inflation, the period when the test is made, and so on. It can be readily understood that if the poor are to be identified by the use of a constant market basket, without allowance being made for a rising standard of living, then poverty will be statistically eliminated in time. As a matter of fact, Victor Fuchs in a study entitled *The Concept of Poverty*, published in 1965, concluded that the incidence of poverty had not changed at all during the postwar period and that statistics to the contrary were just so much sleight of hand. The government had lifted the curse of poverty from millions of Americans (who were still poor) by using outdated statistical assumptions.

Thus, people who were defined as poor in 1972, by the official government standard, were poorer compared with the rest of the population than they had been in earlier years. In 1959, for instance, those defined as poor had about half as much income as the typical family; in 1972, they had only a little more than one-third as much.

With that introduction, we are now ready to place on exhibit several measures of poverty.

Each year, with a great fanfare, the Census Bureau announces a new federal "poverty level" together with an enumeration of the number of Americans existing below standard. The year 1972, for instance, registered the first decline since 1969 in the total number of poor people in America—24.5 million people against 25.6 million a year earlier. This was the number of persons living in families with incomes below the newly established poverty threshold of $4,275 for an urban family of four-up $138 from 1971. ($4,510 in 1974). After another drop in 1973, recession year 1974 saw the number of poor again increase 1.3 million to 24.3 million.

This earlier decrease was accomplished because of a ten percent increase in Social Security benefits that took effect on 1 January 1972 and benefited mostly older and white citizens. The number of poor blacks actually increased by 300,000 during the year, from 7.4 million to 7.7 million. Thus, in 1972, nine percent of all white persons were living in poverty while thirty-three percent of all blacks were in that category.

It should be understood that the dollar increase in the 1972 poverty level, like every annual increase in the poverty definition since 1959, when statistics were first compiled, accounts for inflation, as measured by the Consumer Price Index, and not for an upward revision of the necessities involved in the American standard of living. The poverty level thus includes the barest, elemental requirements to keep body and soul still breathing based on 1959 standards and today's prices. It is a figure that closely approximates the welfare allowance for an urban family of four.

The 1971 estimate of persons below the poverty level, like the 1970 figures, caused some embarrassment because it showed an increase of 200,000 over 1970 and was the highest total since 1967. As a matter of fact, until 1969, the number had dropped annually for a decade, from a total of 39.5 million in 1959—at which time it represented eighteen percent of all families. The 1959 poverty dollar level was $2,973.

The AFL-CIO, in 1971, disputed the Census Bureau calculations, pointing out that the quoted figure of $3,968 would have to go to $4,508 if Social Security and income taxes were added.

Each year, also, the Bureau of Labor Statistics publishes estimates of the amount of money required annually for a higher budget, an intermediate budget, and a low budget standard of living for an urban family of four. The minimum cost for maintaining this typical family during recession year 1974 was $9,200. One out of every four white families, many of them elderly, subsist on incomes beneath the lower level. For blacks, more than half, 59.4 percent, were below it. According to Census Bureau statistics, 35.2 percent of all families had incomes below $9,000 in pre-recession 1972.

The budget-type family studied by the Bureau consists of a thirty-eight-year-old husband employed full time, a non-working housewife, a boy of thirteen and a girl of eight. The lowest budget family lived in rental housing without air-conditioning, performed more services for themselves, and utilized free recreational facilities in the community. Fewer families owned cars at this level and those who did owned older autos. In the model, the family is well established and the husband is an experienced worker—conditions that do not always prevail in true life.

Further, it should be kept in mind that in order to attain even this level of income, a high proportion of families, unlike the sample family studied by the Bureau, needed two or more wage earners. In a study made in 1968, Nicholas Kisburg, legislative and research director for Teamsters Joint Council 16, determined that in white families with incomes in the $5,000 to $6,999 income range, 44.3 percent had two or more wage earners. For incomes of $7,000 to $9,999 the two or more wage earner families represented 56.1 percent. Where there was only one wage earner, half the white families had incomes under $7,283. For similar nonwhite families, the median income was $3,966.

In a study published by the Center for New York City Affairs of the New School for Social Research, it was determined that, in terms of standard budgets for city families developed by the Bureau of Labor Statistics for the spring of 1967, the lowest, but decent, (now called low budget) level represented an income achieved by families averaging 1.49 wage earners, the moderate level involved an average of 1.85 wage earners, and the higher level required 2.19 income earners. The Center concluded: "The wage structure has not, on the average, in the past, permitted the single-earner family to achieve a moderate or high standard of living, and it is not likely to do so for some years to come."

That these statistics have more than theoretical impact was brought home with full force to millions of Americans with the 1971 Phase Two controls. Congress, in Title II, Section 203 (d) of the Economic Stabilization Act of 1971 provided that, "Wage increases to an individual whose earnings are substandard or who is amongst the working poor shall not be limited."

The legislative intent of the Congress was spelled out in the House of Representatives Banking and Currency Committee report that was voted on twenty-nine to zero with two abstentions. It stated that, "this exemption from control applies to all persons whose earnings are at or below levels established by the Bureau of Labor Statistics." This definition, based upon the 1970 low budget estimate at the time, amounted to $6,960.

However, if the intent of the Congress was to have been sustained, more than 50 percent of the nation's workers would have been exempted from the 5.5 percent limit on wage increases. This, or course, could not be. So the Cost of Living Council, through what a New York Times editorial termed "rather tortured arithmetic," performed some "statistical corrections" to reduce the $6,960 "working poor" level to the Government's $3,968 poverty level.

This feat of legerdemain was accomplished by arguing that most families have some income other than the head of the family's regular wage, generally from such sources as overtime work or a working wife, thus giving each family the equivalent of 1.7 workers. Using this standard, by dividing the $6,960 figure by 1.7, the Council came up with an hourly rate of about $1.97 for each worker. And lo and behold, this hourly rate worked out to roughly the poverty level of $3,968 established by the Office of Management and Budget.

Under Phase One, the Council had used the Federal minimum wage of $1.60 an hour that exempted about seven percent of all workers or 5.6 million men and women. Now, under the Phase Two stage, the Council certified to the Pay Board a proposal that earnings of $1.90 an hour or less should be considered substandard and exempt from wage controls. This second figure exempted about fifteen percent of the work force, or 12 million persons. Whereupon, some unions went to court to force the figure up to the Congressional mandate of $3.35 an hour.

Several compromise figures were proposed including one of $2.20 favored by the five public members of the Pay Board that would have put 20 million workers, a quarter of the total, on the exempt list. This compromise was unacceptable to labor. The matter was finally resolved in July 1972 when the Council boosted the wage cutoff for its poverty exemption to $2.75 an hour from $1.90 freeing more than ten million additional workers from wage control for a total of twenty-two million workers, or 27.5 percent of the labor force.

The public discussion of average hourly wage-rates under the economic stabilization program has demonstrated graphically the substandard earnings received by a large segment of the population.

In debate on the minimum wage bill that President Nixon vetoed in 1973 (and signed in 1974) the Senate Labor and Public Welfare Committee estimated that the increase in the minimum (the New York Times calls it the "sub-minimum") wage from $1.60 to $1.80 per hour would mean wage raises for 4.1 million covered workers. The second step increase to $2.00 would cover another 5.5 million workers and a third step increase to $2.20 would raise wages for another 3.6 million workers. In other words, 13.2 million workers of those who would be covered by the ill-fated 1973 legislation were then earning less than $4,576 per annum on a full-time basis. These figures do not reflect the fact that over ten million jobs in the United States are not covered by legislation and pay less than the minimum wage.

These are the working poor. What of the nonworking poor? Statistics for 1975 put the percentage of unemployment for all civilian workers at nine percent, slightly under nine million persons. These are the official figures. Unofficial estimates range as high as ten percent. What is so disturbing about this situation is the ever worsening Phillips Curve—the ineluctable trade-off between unemployment and inflation. Further, any consideration of unemployment statistics must keep in mind that only those available for work are measured. What of those who, in despair, have stopped looking for jobs or who can find only part-time work? The persons who said they wanted jobs but were not looking because they knew they would not find work, the so-called "discouraged workers," number upward of 1,200,000.

These statistics citing the millions of Americans living below the poverty line, eking out an existence below the minimum maintenance level, earning a substandard wage as part of the working poor, unable to find work, have been presented in support of our attempt to explode the myth of

American affluence. Additional proof of the widespread poverty in the United States is the number of persons receiving public welfare.

Despite get-tough administration, tighter eligibility rules, residence requirements, and shifts to Social Security because of higher allowances, the nation's welfare rolls totaled 14.8 million persons in June 1973. During that month, welfare expenditures were running at the annual rate of $22.7 billion. These programs included aid to families with dependent children (the principal form of assistance with 10.9 million recipients), the aged (1.8 million), the blind (80,000), the disabled (over 1.2 million), and the medically indigent. If all forms of assistance at all government levels are included, we arrive at an annual welfare cost of over $35 billion—a staggering sum.

Beginning in January 1974, the Federal Government assumed responsibility for the 3.2 million aged, blind and disabled under the Supplemental Security Income program. The number of eligibles is expected to reach 6.2 million by the end of 1974. Beginning in July of that year, each individual under this program is to receive a minimum monthly cash payment of $140, and each couple $210.

Under the now-abandoned Family Assistance Plan welfare reform program presented by the Nixon administration, a family of four would have been guaranteed an income floor of $2,400. Although this sum is only about one-half of the government starvation level, it is estimated by the Department of Health, Education, and Welfare that adoption of the Administration plan would have added 17.8 million persons and $8.1 billion annually to the welfare rolls by 1977.

Protesting that a $2,400 floor was far too small, Senator Abraham Ribicoff of Connecticut offered a more liberal plan calling for an income floor of $3,000, eventually rising to about $4,000. According to H.E.W. figures, under this plan, some 72.8 million Americans—about a third of the entire population—would receive some measure of welfare subsidy by 1977, at a yearly cost to the Federal government of $41.7

billion. According to Daniel P. Moynihan, the Senator was "genuinely appalled," at these estimates. The demand of the National Welfare Rights Organization for a guaranteed annual income of $5,500 would have covered more than half the population and cost an additional $71 billion.

In the nation's largest city, New York, the 1972-1973 budget of the Human Resources Administration forecasts a case load of 1,340,000—one out of every six persons—at a cost of $2.3 billion. Further, Jule M. Sugarman, the city's Human Resources Administrator, estimated that at least 480,000 people additional are eligible but have not applied because of the stigma. This is corroborated by New York State Commissioner Abe Levine who feared that 300,000 adults would join the welfare rolls when they were federalized and therefore, no longer morally stigmatized. One study found 55.7 percent of New York City's residents—or 4,395,000 persons—to be "deprived."

As mentioned above, the Bureau of Labor Statistics publishes each year estimates for a higher budget, an intermediate budget, and a lower budget. The latest figures for 1974, after the worst inflation in twenty-eight years, indicate that costs for an urban family of four are now $14,300 at an "intermediate level." In the never-ending game of semantics played by the Administration, "intermediate level" had previously been called "moderate level." A review of the components of the so-called "intermediate level" leads one to the conclusion that this level, in fact, represents only a barely adequate standard of living.

To this unsophisticated writer, a family earning less than an amount sufficient to maintain an adequate standard of living is poor.

What percentage of the population, then, earns $14,300 annually or more? For 1974, the Census Bureau reported median income figures for all families as $11,101. This means that half of all families earned more money than this amount before taxes and half earned less. Even this figure is misleading because if we deduct Social Security and income taxes, the mythical middle family only had $10,017 of spendable income left.

The gentle reader who has been doing his arithmetic must be cautioned that the figures cited in this chapter are not cumulative. The same person may be, and probably is, poor, unemployed, and on welfare. Therefore, can we—is it possible—arrive at some intelligent estimate of the extent of poverty in America?

That poverty—dire poverty—actually exists in this richest nation on earth has been established as a fact beyond any question of doubt. No amount of rhetoric, no amount of sweeping the poor under the rug, no semantic change of terminology from poor to low income can hide that fact.

The figures further belie the complacent theories that poverty now exists only in isolated pockets. Paul A. Samuelson, in the 7th Edition of his *Economics: An Introductory Analysis* wrote,

> In the absence of statistical knowledge, it is understandable that one should form an impression of the American standard of living from the full page magazine advertisements portraying a jolly American family in an air conditioned home, with a Buick, a station wagon, a motor launch and all the other good things that go to make up comfortable living. Actually, of course, this sort of life is still beyond the grasp of 90 percent of the American public.

Throughout the Eisenhower years of the 1950s we were told again and again by our social scientists and our public relations men that the poor were no longer with us. Arthur Burns said poverty was only an "intellectual concept" defined by artificial statistics. An earlier John K. Galbraith called poverty "more nearly an afterthought."

Thus, when Michael Harrington in *The Other America: Poverty in the United States* first wrote of forty to fifty million poor in America in 1961 the news was received as startling and even unbelievable. Myths collapsed, shibboliths went tumbling. If anything, Mr. Harrington probably erred at that time on the conservative side. In his most recent book *Socialism,*

Mr. Harrington writes that the statistics prove "that we have in this country a majority composed of the poor, the near poor, more than half the workers and the lower middle class which does not even have a moderate standard of living."

A study published by the University of Michigan in July 1974, indicates that 85 million persons, or forty percent of the nation's population, were eligible for some kind of Federal aid to the poor at some time during the preceding six years.

This writer submits that a fair appraisal of the statistics would indicate that fifteen percent of all Americans, thirty-five million persons, exist below the bread line on the very edge of life, nothing more. Another fifteen percent barely manage to keep body and soul together, living constantly under the pall of family disaster, while a final twenty percent lead lives of structured insecurity in "quiet desperation", teetering on the edge of poverty, being plunged over the precipice upon the occurrence of any emergency such as an illness, an accident, or a recession.

This adds up to fifty percent of the population or one hundred million persons poor or, in Leon Keyserling's phrase, "deprived." The extent of poverty is overwhelming. But we should not be surprised because the basic reality of American life has always been poverty.

Square this with President Nixon's boast that America is "Number 1 in the world economically, the world's most prosperous nation." Square this with President Nixon's statement in 1971 comparing the United States to ancient Greece and Rome; "As they became wealthy, as they lost their will to live, to improve, they became subject to the decadence that destroys the civilization. The United States is reaching that period."

It has been said that statistics do not bleed. Mr. Nixon, the above figures bleed. It is not that a few windows in the great building that is America's economic wealth and might are broken; it is that the foundation, Mr. Nixon, is rotten. How can America call itself capitalist when less than one percent of United States households measure up to Louis O.

Kelso's definition of receiving at least one-half of the annual income spent on consumption in the form of return on invested capital? As long as there is this other America we are, all of us, poorer because of it.

Poverty is much more than a lack of cash, and statistics on poverty can never convey its human meaning. What hunger, what disease, what ignorance, what misery, what humiliation, what corrosion of dignity, what despair, what frustration are hidden in these figures? How many hopes and dreams have been crushed by the grim grip of poverty from which there is no earthly release? How much filth, dirt, vermin, germs, stench, and squalor are latent in these statistics? How many premature deaths, infant mortalities, stunted intellects, wasted lives, lost efforts are there? Millions of our fellow Americans are faced with day to day deprivations that degrade human dignity to levels that no statistics can adequately describe. Powerlessness, too, corrupts. Millions of our fellow Americans endure a condition of life so deformed by disease, illiteracy, malnutrition, and squalor as to deny the victims basic human necessities.

Mr. Harrington replies to those who compare the living standards of the American poor to those of the medieval serfs or Asian peasants. The American poor are not poor in the sixteenth century or in Hong Kong. They are poor here, now, in the United States. Those who suffer levels of life well below those that are possible are poor.

Mr. Harrington pleads with us to forget the numbers game. Whatever the precise calibration of the poverty level, it is obvious that the statistics cited in this chapter represent an enormous, an unconscionable amount of human suffering in this land. They should be read with a sense of outrage.

Henry George stated only too well that, "poverty is not merely deprivation; it means shame, degradation, the searing of the most sensitive parts of our moral and mental nature as with hot irons; the denial of the strongest impulses and the sweetest affections; the wrenching of the most vital nerves." Rosa Guy wrote, "there is no political system that can take away freedom as completely, as relentlessly as prejudice and poverty."

What is so demoralizing is the hopelessness of it all. Despite Mr. Nixon's claim that, "This nation can work its way out of poverty," the Heineman Commission reported that, "Our economic and social structure virtually guarantees poverty for millions of Americans." The poor are the scrap material of our industrial system, existing outside the American money economy. The odds are long against a family's breaking out of the cycle of abject, dependent, rooted poverty, for poverty perpetuates itself, dooming generation after generation to a life of deprivation—a hereditary underclass. The poor become characters in a William Beckett drama with no hope of any resolution except idiotic despair.

Prerevolutionary America should, therefore, be reminded of Sir Francis Bacon's observation that the worst rebellions are belly rebellions. It was President Kennedy who warned, "If America cannot provide for the many who are poor, how can it protect the few who are rich?" It was also President Kennedy who quoted Seneca: "A hungry people listens not to reason, nor cares for justice, nor is bent by prayers," A nation cannot survive half engulfed in misery, half enjoying fat-dripping prosperity. Wise Adam Smith warned two centuries ago that, "No society can surely be flourishing and happy, of which the far greater part of the members are poor and miserable."

John Steinbeck wrote in *Grapes Of Wrath*, "The fields were fruitful and starving men moved on the roads. The granaries were full and the children of the poor grew up richitic and the postules of pallagra swelled on their sides. . . and in the eyes of the people there is a failure and in the eyes of the hungry there is a growing wrath."

Extreme economic inequality leads to extreme social tensions; teeming, hungry, combustible human beings, counted in the millions, are awakening to a nation that offers so much for all but presents to little to them. Lord Boyd Orr of Brechin warned, "Hunger is the greatest of all politicians and hungry mobs don't care two hoots about political theories. They will tear down any government which cannot provide food and will follow any demagogue who promises it."

"It shall come to pass, that when they shall be hungry, they shall fret themselves and curse their king and their God."

3

The Victims

It becomes clear that poverty is a disease that is endemic in the United States. The festering sores of that disease are manifest across the breadth of the land in widespread hunger, decaying slums, pesthole hospitals, dying schools, and faded citizens whose mainsprings have been broken.

What are we doing to combat this terrible disease?

Senator Robert Kennedy spoke passionately of a "generous and compassionate country." David Reisman wrote in *The Lonely Crowd*, "There is a great generosity among Americans." The traditional American democratic sense of fair play has commonly exhibited a regard for those in need, respect for the integrity of the individual, and compassion for fellow humans. We had been reared in the belief that it was important to keep alive in the hearts of our less fortunate neighbors some shred of human decency, some spark of humanity, some hope that all good had not vanished from the earth. We were imbued with the sanctity, the worth, and the dignity of each of God's creatures.

What has happened to the great heart of America?

There is an old Indian proverb that states, "God we shall see in the smile of the poor." But such a regard for those less fortunate is no longer fashionable. Instead of viewing increased welfare rolls as an achievement of reaching the people who need the assistance, we are ashamed of them. Our attitude toward welfare recipients has turned to outright hostility and they are subjected to unmerciful calumny and abuse. The hue and cry of the pack in cruel and callous pursuit of a handful of relief malingerers is symptomatic of a sadistic streak in our national character. A survey conducted in November 1973 by Daniel Yankelovich, Inc. found that sixty-one percent of New Yorkers believed that that city was overly kind to welfare recipients.

Give to bankrupt railroads, failing defense contractors, shipping interests, grain dealers, milk producers, and the like. That is not welfare; that is strengthening the economy. Send a CARE package to Biafra or Bangladesh and you are hailed a humanitarian. But advocate feeding the hungry in your home town and you are denounced as a Communist. The in-phrase now is "work ethic"—not "welfare ethic." For welfare has acquired a sinister meaning; it has become an evil word, a term of debasement.

The Republican Party national platform for 1972 flatly opposed programs that embrace the principle of a government guaranteed income, and rejected as unconscionable the idea that all citizens have the right to be supported by the government.

We have all heard the myths about the able-bodied men sitting around drunk and lazy on welfare. We can cite, until we are blue in the face, statistics to prove that 55.5 percent of the people on welfare are children under eighteen; 25 percent are blind, aged, or disabled; 18.6 percent are mothers; less than 1 percent are able-bodied men; 68 percent of the children were born in wedlock. Suspected welfare fraud occurs in less than four-tenths of one percent of the nation's total welfare case load. The largest racial group among welfare families—49 percent—is white.

A careful social psychological study, *Do The Poor Want To Work?* by Leonard Goodwin of the Brookings Institution comes up with findings that differ sharply from the commonly accepted stereotyped concept of the poor. Based on interviews with a large sample of persons of all colors, sexes, and ages—working and jobless—the study concludes that welfare recipients, whatever their race or time spent on the welfare rolls, have essentially the same work ethic and life aspirations as do employed middle-class individuals.

A similar study, commissioned by the Department of Labor and conducted by Louis A. Ferman, research director of the Institute of Labor and Industrial Relations at the University of Michigan, and Joe A. Miller, now of Pennsylvania State University, determined that most of what the public thinks about welfare recipients is a stereotype with little basis in fact.

What these welfare recipients lack is confidence. George Orwell described how those who wanted work desperately but could not find it were "haunted by a feeling of personal degradation." But who is interested in such social-psychological studies? Who is interested in the statistics?

Rather, we want to be insulated from the miseries of our fellows. We retreat to our ivory towers and blot out the fearful spectacle of human misery, the haunting voices of abject poverty. We hide our poor out of sight in the shadows of the slums and in the tar-paper shacks of the countryside. There is an increasingly deliberate attempt to slide the poor out of the very experience and consciousness of the nation. As C.P. Snow stated, "we draw the curtains."

We even blot the evil word "poor" out of our dictionaries as a nonword and substitute the so-called "more professional term" devoid of emotional complications of "low income population." George H. Brown, director of the Census Bureau, explains that the new term does not have "the stereoptical image," as has the value-laden concept of that nasty word "poverty". Poor children, too, have disappeared, if not from the slums, then at least from the language. First, they became, "deprived," and then "disadvantaged." Shades of George Orwell's Newspeak.

Shane Stevens writes,

> I have been through most of the big towns and most of the smaller cities of this affluent society of ours. I have seen the hungry people. They are easy to see except for the fact that they are invisible. They're the ones you pass on the streets, your eyes straight ahead. They're the ones you dump into shacks on the other side of town or herd into slums. They're the ones you curse for wasting your tax money.

Margaret Mead told the Senate Labor and Public Welfare subcommittee in September 1973, "Richest and strongest nation we may be, but we seem to have lost any concern for those who are young or weak, old or poor." She added that America has slid into, "a pit of deterioration, corruption, apathy, indifference and outright brutality towards the weak, the sick, the young and the poor."

The Good Book states, "The righteous considereth the cause of the poor but the wicked regardeth not to know it."

Who are the victims of this policy of callous indifference and brutality?

First among these victims are those who hunger.

For the first obligation of any nation is to provide food for all of its citizens. This obligation overrides all political, economic, racial, religious, social, or age differences. In March 1975 the chief executive officers of the nation's three major religions declared that eating is "a fundamental human right." Yet the United States government has officially admitted that millions of Americans go hungry. President Nixon was perturbed by the situation. On 6 May 1969, he pledged to put "an end to hunger in America for all times. Something very like the honor of American democracy is at issue," he said.

But five years later, in June 1974, a panel of specialists reported to the Senate Select Committee on Nutrition and Human Needs that, "over the past three to four years, our nation's needy have become hungrier and poorer."

Although twenty-one million persons, at a cost of $6 billion annually, receive a food subsidy from the government that is admittedly inadequate to cover the cost of a basic economy diet, the above Senate committee estimated, in March 1975, that only thirty-eight percent of those eligible for food stamps were getting them.

Holding that the evidence presented had proven that the needs of millions of persons remained unmet, Federal district Judge Miles Lord, in October, 1974, ordered the Department of Agriculture to spend the $278 million remaining from the 1973 fiscal food stamp budget instead of returning the money to the Treasury. This surplus remained despite the outreach provisions of the Food Stamp Act of 1971.

In June 1975, the United States Court of Appeals held that food stamp benefits were too low to provide even the Department of Agriculture's economy plan diet.

The toll of hunger and poverty is reflected in the health of the poor. A survey made by Louis Harris in 1968 reported that the poor person was four times more likely to suffer from a heart condition than a high income person, six times more likely to suffer from arthritis and rheumatism, six times more likely to have high blood pressure, three times more likely to have orthopedic impairment, and eight times more likely to have visual impairment. August B. Hollingshead and F.C. Redlich, based upon a 1958 survey in New Haven, Connecticut, concluded that three times as many poor had psychiatric illnesses as did persons in upper income groups.

The results of a two-year study by the Meharry Medical College of the effectiveness of health services for poor families in Nashville, Tennessee, concluded in October 1974, found that only thirteen percent of those in 1,266 households with diagnosed medical problems were receiving the appropriate medical care.

Here too, the myth of the affluent America clouds the comprehension of the scope of ill health in the United States. For instance, when Congress adopted the medicaid program in 1965 it had no idea of how much the cost would be. The initial projection was $238 million annually. Actually, in 1975, closer to $15 billion was being spent.

Another set of prime victims of the policy of callous indifference and brutality are the children who live in poverty. Obviously, they are the most vulnerable of the population and they suffer most from being locked into a life of guaranteed poverty. It is the children who must give us great concern for they are the proven reserves of the nation's human resources.

One-sixth of our nation's 62.7 million children under the age of sixteen and one out of every four children under the age of six live at or below the poverty line. At least one-half of the children suffer from some form of malnutrition. One-fourth of all children, ages five to fourteen, have never seen a dentist.

Dr. Charles Upton Lowe, Jr., chairman of the Committee on Nutrition of the American Academy of Pediatrics, estimates that a poor child is twice as likely to succumb to infant mortality as a high income child, at least ten times more likely to suffer mental retardation, four times more likely to be the hapless victim of maternal mortality, twice as likely to be born premature, and twice as likely to suffer chronic illness. Thirty-seven percent are fated to live in households headed by a woman, with all that that status implies. One-fourth of the mothers giving birth each year have little or no obstetric care.

A parallel survey by the National Children's Bureau entitled *From Birth to Seven*, of 17,000 children born in one week in 1958 found that, by the age of seven, working-class youngsters have dropped far behind their middle-class contemporaries in reading, school work, and mental development.

Approximately 740,000 children are born into poverty each year. Nearly fourteen million children are growing up today in families that statistically cannot afford to feed them properly. They go to bed hungry, not having enough protein to build a healthy brain, and condemned to remain half-human all their lives. For we know that the first year is very important in the life of an infant; the brain size is pretty well fixed by that time. According to the American Association for the

Advancement of Science, a hungry child, by the age of three, may have fallen permanently behind better-nourished youngsters even though the hungry child started out with better mental potential. According to Dr. Lowe, the quality and quantity of nutrition given during the first four years may have the effect of programming a child for life.

Square this situation with President Nixon's pledge of "a national commitment to providing all American children an opportunity for healthful and stimulating development during the first five years of life."

The President's proposed ill-fated H.R. 1, in effect, would have forced mothers, especially unmarried mothers, to register for full-time work or job training, or else be stricken from the welfare rolls. In 1971, forty-three percent of the nation's mothers worked outside the home. This is an expensive way of depressing welfare rolls. It will be paid for in terms of the impoverishment of home life, at the expense of hundreds of thousands of children who will receive less care, love, and supervision. We have mortgaged the future. It is cheaper to feed and nurture the child than to jail the man.

Nor has child labor been effaced from the land. In 1971 the Department of Labor reported that more than one-fourth of the country's seasonal farm work force—roughly 800,000 out of 3.1 million—were children under the age of sixteen, laboring usually under the most appalling of work conditions. Of these, almost half were between ten and thirteen. The American Friends Service Committee made a five-state study of child labor and concluded, "The child labor scene in the 1970's is reminiscent of the sweatshop scene in 1938."

Millions of our children grow up in a state of continual desperation. They are born without hospitals, nurtured often without milk and insufficient food, schooled without love, indoctrinated without learning, and grow to their tormented manhood without the care of a pediatrician, dentist, or oculist.

The United States has formulated in words its obligations to its children by ratifying the Declaration of the Rights of the

Child, which was adopted by the fourteenth session of the United Nations General Assembly in 1959. It is ironic to square that resolution against the existing state of facts. The Declaration states: "Mankind owes to the child the best it has to give to the end that he may have a happy childhood." Principle six goes on to say, "The child needs love and understanding. He shall...grow up...in an atmosphere of affection and...security."

We also find our victims at the other limit of the age spectrum. Their condition is equally pathetic. We speak of old age that Ralph Nader calls, "the last segregation." Senior Citizen is a patronizing term for our elderly who are used so brutally.

There are 20.6 million Americans aged sixty-five or older, and 40 percent of them are poor. Eleven percent of elderly families and 53 percent of elderly individuals received less than $30 weekly, including Social Security benefits. Another 30 percent of each category received between $30 and $60 weekly. 1.3 million persons must receive Old Age Assistance in addition to Social Security.

In other societies, the elderly are honored. Only in the United States do we seek to segregate the aging by shoving them into stinking storage bins euphoniously called nursing home or rest places. Very little attention has been devoted in this country to relieving the economic problems of the aging, who are finding it increasingly difficult to live in dignity with shrinking incomes in a youth-oriented society.

The 71st Psalm reads, "Cast me not away in the time of old age. Forsake me not when my strength faileth." This plea has fallen upon deaf ears in America. Charles de Gaulle was more realistic. "Old age is a shipwreck," he said.

4

More Victims

Yes, the victims are legion.

Quite clearly, the victims sinned against the most by American society are the blacks. So much has been written by so many authorities on the dilemma of the blacks in America that a lengthy dissertation would be presumptuous.

Suffice it to state that although the racist statutes may have been stricken down and the Negro may have achieved legal equality in the schools, in the courts, on the voting rolls, and on the buses, he is still left with the poverty that is the historic and institutionalized consequence of color. To quote Frederick Douglass, the black man was left, "free to hunger; free to the winter and the rains of heaven...free without roofs to cover them or bread to eat...We gave them freedom and famine at the same time. The marvel is that they still live."

The black winds up with a mouthful of civil rights and an empty stomach. What good does it do to be able to eat at a lunch counter if you cannot buy a hamburger? The answer to that question is the basis for Rev. Jesse L. Jackson's Operation PUSH to substitute a "civil economic movement" for the "civil rights movement."

As stated above, the median income for white families reached $13,500 in 1974, while for the usually larger black family it was $7,800 or fifty-eight percent of the whites. Nonwhite unemployment in 1975 was fifteen percent of the work force, almost double the rate for whites, while the jobless rate for black teenagers registered an unbelievable 41.5 percent, a statistic that is real social dynamite. High unemployment here spawns many other evils, particularly in the ghetto where there is an obvious relationship between scarcity of jobs and crime and drug addiction. The percentage of housing with inadequate plumbing occupied by blacks remained at about thirty percent during the 1960s. Sixty-two percent of nonwhites reside in hard-core slums. Black life expectancy at birth is 6.6 years less than whites. The black infant mortality rate is twice that of whites. One-quarter of all black families received some form of public assistance in 1971 compared with five percent of white families.

Black Americans, comprising 11.3 percent of the population, possess, according to economist Henry S. Terrell, only 1.2 percent of the total United States wealth. Blacks own only 0.1 percent of the value of all stock holdings. Black businesses had receipts in 1972 representing only three-tenths of one percent of the total business receipts of the nation. Black banks control only one-fiftieth of one percent of the banking assets of the nation. Bayard Rustin stated, "The term black capitalism doesn't mean a thing to the black masses. It only means that the middle class blacks get richer."

In 1971, 34.8 percent of persons arrested for violent crimes were blacks. A study by University of Pennsylvania criminologists indicated that 50.2 percent of black boys born in Philadelphia in 1945 were arrested at least once before the age of nineteen. Of the 4.8 million black families in the nation, 1.5 million, or 32 percent are households headed by women, compared with 9 percent of white families. For 1971, the high school dropout rate for blacks were 11.1 percent against 7.4 percent for whites.

The crisis of the black man is caused not so much by the transition from slavery to equality as by a change from an economics of exploitation to an economics of uselessness. The blacks have not been brought out of the cotton fields into the main stream of constructive work activity. Further, as automation steadily wipes out thousands of unskilled and semi-skilled jobs each year, we find that the black is the worker who is displaced.

Thus, the black's real problem is not so much racial discrimination, per se, but that he is becoming permanently unemployed. Because of his lack of education and preparation, the black does not get far enough along in the hiring process to find out if discrimination exists.

The great mass of blacks are locked in a permanent condition of poverty, trapped in inherited gateless misery. In the words of President Johnson,

> They lack training and skills. They are shut in slums without decent medical care. Private and public poverty combine to cripple their capacities. . .In far too many ways American Negroes have been another nation, deprived of freedom, crippled by hatred, the doors of opportunity closed to hope.

No progress will be made towards resolving the dilemma of the twentieth century until it is recognized that the blacks in truth constitute another nation—an underdeveloped nation—in our midst. The National Advisory Commission on Civil Disorders, headed by Otto Kerner, termed us "two nations, separate and unequal."

Martin Luther King, Jr. once had a dream. Langston Hughes asks, "What happens to a dream deferred?"

Does it dry up
Like a raisin in the sun?
Or fester like a sore—
And then run?
Does it stink like rotten meat
or crust and sugar over—
Like a syrupy sweet?
Maybe it just sags
Like a heavy load
Or does it explode?

There is a three hundred-year-old bill that is due and that has to be paid. What will happen when it is presented for payment?

The black asks only a fair share of the American pie. Gwendolyn Brooks best expressed this plaint:

> Grant me that I am human, that I hurt,
> That I can cry.
> Nor that I now asks alms, in shame gone hollow,
> Nor cringe outside the loud and sumptuous gate,
> Admit me to our mutual estate.

Or are the Black Liberation Army and the Symbionese Liberation Army the only possible response?

Nor do the blacks make up the lowest rung of the underclass. Conditions are even worse among the other darker-skinned victims: Puerto Ricans, Chicanos and American Indians.

Of the 11.2 million persons of Spanish origin in the United States, 5.2 percent of the nation's population, many were in the lower paying occupations. Median family income for 1974 was $9,559, compared with $12,836 for all families. 2.6 million Hispanic persons lived below the poverty level.

In the area of education, Spanish-speaking Americans were far behind blacks and whites with only thirty-five percent completing four years of high school or more, compared with sixty-five percent of all blacks and ninety percent of white Americans.

The American Indian, an alien in his own land, the poorest minority group in America, has not yet come to the end of his "Trail of Tears." That what white America has done to the Indian amounts to genocide may be inferred not only from the small number of Indians left alive today (792,730 in 1970), but from the half-life thrust upon them—an infant mortality rate and a suicide rate twice the national average; a life expectancy of forty-seven years; an annual median family income of $5,832; an average of five years in wretched schools; an unemployment rate of 45 percent; and the Bureau of Indian Affairs. For every twelve Indians, there is one Indian Affairs bureaucrat; for nine-hundred Indians, one doctor.

Based on the 1970 census, the Indian lagged behind the rest of the nation in just about every socio-economic barometer. Nearly forty percent of the Indian population lived below the Federal poverty level in 1969. Assimilate or starve! This has been the choice offered to the Indian. One begins to understand the seizure of Wounded Knee, South Dakota, by the militants of the American Indian Movement.

For instance, let us look at the Navajos. On 1 June 1868, after a merciless campaign by Kit Carson's troops, the Navajos signed a treaty committing their future to the United States government. In October 1973, the United States Commission on Civil Rights reported on the results of that treaty. It found the 137,000 Navajos to be impoverished, exploited, and near bankruptcy, despite valuable natural resources. Per capita income is under $1,000 a year—on a par with Malaysia. Sixty percent of their dwellings have no electricity; eighty percent no water or sewers. The median educational level is 5.3 years against a national level of 12.1 years. A staggering fifty-six percent were unemployed and alcoholism was rampant. Read the 1975 report of the Federal Commission on Civil Rights: *The Navajo Nation: An American Colony.*

No enumeration of victims, of the disaffected, the oppressed, the exploited, and the discontented is complete without the inclusion of fifty-one percent of our population—women. By every statistical measure, women must also be counted with the underclass.

Theodore and Betty Roszak wrote in *Masculine/Feminine,*

> For the truth is that women are members of a caste, socially dispersed by the family system, but collectively victimized by a life-long process of sexual stereotyping contrived to make the world safe for male supremacy. That is the plain fact of life.

A special Presidential committee reported that for 1968, the median full time earnings of white men was $7,396, of black men $4,777, of white women $4,279, and of black women $3,194. Women with some college education, both white and black, earned less than black men with eight years of education.

The earnings gap was apparent throughout a wide spectrum of jobs. For instance, the median wage for women sales workers was $3,461, while for men it was $8,549. Women who were full university professors were earning $11,649; men received $12,768. A report prepared by the Women's Bureau of the Department of Labor showed that for 1970 only seven percent of working women earned more than $10,000 a year against forty percent for men. Twelve percent of women earned less than $3,000 while only five percent of the men earned that little. The Bureau found that the gap in earnings between the sexes had widened in fifteen years. In 1955 the median wage of the working American woman was nearly sixty-four percent of her male counterpart; in 1970, only 59.4 percent. Further, not only did women receive unequal pay for equal work, they were also employed in the less-skilled and lower-paying jobs.

Does the women's liberation movement conjure up visions of Madam La Farge knitting while the tumbrils roll?

Our role call of victims is far from ended. Our Republic always recognized the role of the farmer as the bulwark of our system of government. Countless laws favor the farmer through subsidies, price supports, crop limitations, scientific assistance, rail rates, marketing aids, etc., etc.

Yet, the past thirty years has witnessed the almost complete obliteration of the farm population. The technical revolution has forced a radical change in the whole face of farming. It has replaced men with machines in field and barn. It has added vastly to productivity with costly fertilizers, pesticides, and new seed varieties.

Since 1940, nearly twenty-one million people have been forced to leave the farms. In that period the farm population has dropped from 30.5 million, or 23.2 percent of the toal population, to 9.7 million, or only 4.8 percent of the total. The number of farms has dropped from 6.35 million to 2.82 million while the average acreage per farm has more than doubled from 167 acres to 387 acres. Empty houses and weed-overgrown yards dot the countryside.

The median annual money income of families and unrelated individuals residing on farms in 1969 was $6,385, well below the national median and the low budget standard discussed earlier. For the 1.4 million hired farm laborers who were displaced from their farms and reduced to the status of serfs, the average annual wage for 1970 came to only $1,576.

Factories in the field have taken over. Corporate farming has become the dominant force in rural America. Control of agriculture has moved from the fields to the board rooms of New York. By way of illustration, Tenneco, the nation's thirty-fourth largest corporation, which owns or leases more than a million acres in the West, plows its land with tractors manufactured by one of its subsidiaries, sprays its crops with pesticides from another, and processes, packages, and sells its products through still other companies within the same corporate structure. In 1964, 6.6 percent of commercial farms accounted for almost fifty percent of all farm marketings, two percent for more than one-third of all farm sales.

A suit filed in October 1972 by the Migrant Legal Action Program, Inc., a public interest law association, accused the Department of Agriculture, among others, of catering to the interests of the large agriculture corporations.

Who will man the National Guard and the Army when there are no farm boys? Oliver Goldsmith phrased it very well:

Ill fares the land, to hastening ills a prey,
Where wealth accumulates, and men decay;
Princes and lords may flourish or may fade;
A breath can make them, as a breath has made;
But a bold peasantry, their country's pride,
When once destroy'd, can never be supplied.

The most abused of our victims are the prisoners, shut out of sight, less than humans.

Dr. Martin Groder, director of the Federal Center for Correctional Research at Camp Butner, North Carolina, regards the prison system as a sort of last ditch welfare system—at a cost of about $6,000 per year per man—for young healthy males who are otherwise ineligible for most regular welfare programs but who do not have the skills or the opportunity to earn a living. Jessica Mitford, author of *Kind and Unusual Punishment: The Prison Business*, estimates that it costs as much to keep a man in San Quentin as it would be to send him to Harvard.

Unable to make a go of things on the outside, the exconvict returns to his refuge—the prison. A study by the Federal Bureau of Investigation showed that about two-thirds of all persons released from prison were rearrested within four years.

Drug addiction may also thus be better understood as a symbol of separation and alienation from the dominant values of American society.

We did not need Attica to demonstrate to us that our prisons are a disgrace. The recidivism rate for all youthful offenders is seventy-four percent. Dostoevsky wrote, in the *House of the Dead,* "The degree of civilization in a society can be judged by entering its prisons."

These are our human victims. But the scars imposed by America sit also on our physical environment.

Where do our poor live? Congress declared in 1948 that the national goal was "a decent home and a suitable living environment for every American family." We dreamed of a "city on a hill, the city, the hope of democracy."

Twenty-three years later, the Lindsay-Harris commission found that, "Housing is still the national scandal it was then." To be honest, housing conditions in the slums have been a national scandal for 125 years. Charles Dickens, in a visit to black homes in New York's Five Points area in 1842, found them to be "leprous houses," "hideous tenements," and "cramped hutches," lacking minimal comforts.

Our rat and roach infested tenements of today match these descriptions. Today, almost two million New Yorkers live in depressing, decaying housing. Three hundred thousand "Old Law" tenement units in 40,000 buildings, usually with only one toilet on each floor, and interior rooms open only to air shafts, are still standing and house more than a million people although such construction was outlawed in 1901. At least another 200,000 "New Law" tenement units—one-quarter of those built between 1901 and 1929—which were neglected during forty years of depression, war, and rent control, require replacement or total rehabilitation. Still another one hundred thousand prohibited single-room occupancy units without bathrooms are also in use.

A 1972 *New York Times* survey and analysis of housing showed general agreement among housing and planning officials that the great majority of New Yorkers, perhaps more than seventy percent, can no longer afford unsubsidized housing. Yet, Congress never funded the program it voted in 1949 of 810,000 new public-housing units in the next six years, while public housing accounts for only one percent of all housing in the United States compared to twenty percent in Britain.

A housing study conducted by Drs. Bernard J. Frieden and David Birch for the M.I.T.-Harvard Joint Center, classified 13.1 million families, 21 percent of the 63.4 households in 1970, as "housing deprived."

Former Vice President Spiro Agnew admitted to a New York Building Congress luncheon that the country's low and middle income housing programs had been "a costly failure" because only one of every fifteen persons eligible for housing assistance had actually been helped. President Nixon called for scrapping the entire existing program because it benefited the real estate speculator rather than the citizen.

We have allowed the rot to eat into the core of our cities. Every element of neglect, squalor, decay, filth, crime, disease, and futility that one can imagine finds its repository in the slum. Our inner cities are true disaster areas; even the slum lords are abandoning them.

We find a segregated two-class hospital system in every big city. There are private hospitals with modern technology and personal nursing care for the rich, and understaffed municipal hospitals with beds in the corridors and crowded wooden benches in the clinics for the poor. Dr. Samuel Rubin likens New York's city hospitals to "outhouses in the Ozarks."

Mayor Kenneth A. Gibson of Newark charged, "We have tens of thousands of poor persons here who do not receive any kind of decent medical care." The country is short 30,000 doctors.

Believe it or not, our wealthy United States, in 1969, ranked thirty-fifth among world nations in life expectancy for men and sixteenth for women, while our infant mortality rate was inferior to that of twenty-one other countries. Our mothers die in child birth at a rate exceeding eleven other countries. Half of all draftees were rejected by the armed forces due to lack of physical fitness.

Schools and libraries are in scandalously short supply. While existing schools are ramshackle and delapidated, the country needs something like 140,000 more classrooms. The Carnegie Corporation estimates that 200,000 talented high school graduates cannot afford college. The Office of Education estimated in October 1969 that there were more than twenty million functional illiterates in the United States.

A 1966 study showed that 18.7 percent of all white recruits taking the Armed Forces Qualification Test for induction failed, while 67.2 percent of all black recruits failed to make the grade. In a United States armed forces program, called Project 100,000 more than 68 percent of the participants fell below grade seven in reading and academic ability.

Dr. Mark R. Shedd, superintendent of the Philadelphia school system told the Senate Select Committee on Equal Education Opportunity on 21 September 1971 that the urban schools of this country were dying from financial strangulation.

We suffer every day with rickety commuter transportation. Our clogged city streets are impassable. We forget that one of the causes of the Watts riot was that only one bus line ran to the area of opportunity in Los Angeles.

We wrote above about the need for housing. But as Henry Thoreau asked, "What is the use of a house if you haven't got a tolerable planet to put it on?" We poison the land, befoul the water, erode natural resources, and imperil the public health. In three and a half centuries we have plundered a land that took tens of thousands of years to form. Stewart L. Udall wrote in *The Quiet Crisis*, "we raided the Indians, raided the continent and raided the future." To think that Richard Hakluyt, the eighteenth-century English historian, called America, "the goodliest land under the cope of heaven."

Barry Commoner writes in *The Closing Circle*, "despite its apparent prosperity, in reality the system is being driven into bankruptcy. Environmental deterioration represents a crucial, potentially fatal, hidden factor in the operation of the economic system."

We inhabit what Anne Lindbergh calls, "a dying environment that is encroaching on us like a lava flow." Industrial vomit, the fecal matter of our civilization, fills our skies and seas. Remember that there were once cedars in Lebanon and fertile areas in the Sahara. Don Marquis' archy writes to Mehitabel, "it won't be long now it won't be long till earth is barren as the moon and sapless as a mumbled bone..." Man must be considered an endangered species like the whooping crane.

Consider the Great Lakes, the world's largest body of fresh water. At the beginning of the century, the condition of the lakes did not differ greatly from that of eleven thousand years ago when the glaciers retreated. Today, Lake Erie is virtually dead—a cesspool; no fish live there. Lake Michigan and the others are on their way to the same fate. It has been estimated that if all human polluting activity were to halt immediately, it would require about five hundred years to restore Lake Erie to its condition of twenty-five years ago and about one hundred years to bring Lake Michigan back—if indeed this was possible at all.

Dr. William H. Harris of Brooklyn College found sewage sludge as close as a half-mile off Atlantic Beach on the south shore of Long Island.

In Los Angeles, New York, and a dozen other cities, our lungs gasp for a breath of clean air. We are becoming people without a country.

These, we, are the victims. In its headlong haste to milk technology for immediate economic advantage, the one percent of the population who owns America has left in its wake huge slag piles of human and ecological debris. We have left the poor, marginal, and unskilled human flotsam, rejected and despised, hungry, subject to a lifetime of abuse and indignity, set outside of the bounds of society by an unbroken cycle of poverty. We have left the young alienated, turned off, frustrated, resentful. We have left the blacks and other nonwhites discriminated against, exploited, imprisoned in ghettos, harassed by authority, suppressed. We have left the women newly awakened to their inferior caste position. We have left the aged forsaken, neglected, embittered, ill. We have left the children ill-fed, ill-treated, miseducated, abused, abandoned. We—all of us, rich and poor—inhabit a polluted land that has been so destroyed and desecrated that it no longer provides a suitable place for human habitation.

In our two hundred years of independence, we have succeeded in converting the United States of America into a social and physical tinderbox that threatens to explode like an atom bomb. John Kenneth Galbraith has warned that the continued neglect of the public sector could result in social eruption. Our society has truly entered the phase of self-destruct. A single spark can light a prairie fire.

Two hundred years of independence, let us hope, has not blotted out our dream of Liberty, Equality, Fraternity. Liberty evokes a need; Fraternity an ideal; but Equality stakes a claim, utters a protest, forecasts a rebellion. It is at the root of the struggle for social justice.

5

Where Has All the Money Gone?

This author happened to have been in Mexico City during the 1930s when it was impossible to walk the streets at night because of the people sleeping on the sidewalks. When he asked why, the answer was very simple: Because they had no money.

Why do we have poverty and hunger, slums, crumbling schools, decaying cities, outhouse hospitals, filthy streets, and pollution? The answer is again very simple: Because there is no money.

What is the magic wand that will wipe out the ills of our society? What will smother the glowing coals of rebellion in our society? The magic wand, the answer is *money*.

But the price will not be cheap. Vast sums of money are required to remedy the maladies enumerated in the previous chapters.

We must recognize that we will never achieve a decent human society in America by patching up symptoms; by treating rat bites and ignoring the rats; by distributing food stamps and ignoring the root causes of hunger; by stockpiling guns for the police while ignoring the real crime in our streets.

The March 1971 issue of *Fortune Magazine* stated that the response of the United States to social problems was that of "a second rate nation with a civilization only half built." *Fortune's* editors offered a program for the rehabilitation of the nation's people and resources that included spending a total of $57 billion a year on nine priority areas: $18 billion for education, $10 billion for medical care, $12 billion for welfare reforms, $6.5 billion for the inner cities, $3 billion to control suburban sprawl, $2.5 billion to combat air and water pollution, $2 billion for mass transit, $2 billion for crime control, and $1 billion to rehabilitate strip mines, melt junk cars, and remove highway billboards.

Studies published by the Brookings Institution and the National Urban Coalition arrive at $96 billion as the necessary approximate increase needed annually during the next decade to meet commonly agreed upon targets of social betterment. Of this, $30 billion is earmarked for housing, $20 billion for education, $20 billion for health care, $12 billion for law enforcement and improvements to the penal and judicial systems, $10 billion for pollution control, and $4 billion for mass transit. This amount would represent a 55.2 percent increase over the $174 billion actually spent in these categories during 1970.

In addition, Joseph A. Pechman, director of economic studies at the Brookings Institution, estimated annual costs of $7.2 billion for child development, $59 billion for national health insurance, $4 billion for urban redevelopment, $6 billion for rural redevelopment, and $9 billion for public service employment so that the government might act as the employer of last resort. Add day-care centers and you need another $20 billion annually.

As noted above, a *New York Times* survey showed general agreement among housing and planning officials that the great majority of New Yorkers, perhaps more than seventy percent, can no longer afford unsubsidized housing. To replace the bad housing in New York City alone would cost $25 billion. California needs 500,000 new housing units; the nation at large at least 6.9 million new units. Under today's income and asset limits, approximately forty percent of the population is eligible for subsidized housing, yet only a small fraction lives in such units. Only fifteen percent of the families can afford to buy a new home.

In his farewell to the Department of Health, Education and Welfare, Secretary Elliot L. Richardson declared that "to extend the present range of H.E.W. services equitably to those in need would require seemingly impossible allocations of resources—an additional twenty million trained personnel and an additional $250 billion, a sum equal to the entire Federal budget." He continued, "The legislative process has become a cruel shell game and the service system has become a bureaucratic maze, inefficient, incomprehensible and inaccessible."

The infrastructure—power, communication, and transportation—of the cities is in disrepair. The housing stock is decaying and basic public services like sewer, water, and waste treatment, require immense investments. But the city and state budgets are already hopelessly overtaxed. The special commission established by the National Urban Coalition concluded that if present trends continue, "most cities by 1980 will be preponderantly black and brown, and totally bankrupt." Witness New York City.

The Council on Environmental Quality estimated that it would cost at least $274 billion over the next decade to solve the country's major pollution problems. Barry Commoner fixes the price tag at a much higher figure. He estimates that the United States must spend more than $40 billion annually on ecological reconstruction over the next generation if we are not to suffer disaster.

There is no money, so the nation is short 30,000 doctors and nine million jobs. There is no money, so libraries and schools are forced to close in Ohio, in Gary, in Detroit, and elsewhere. Ferdinand Lundberg writes, "It seems extremely strange to me to curtail valuable library services in a country that has a gross national product of a trillion dollars."

There is no money, so the nation's cultural facilities are falling into ruin. August Heckscher, the administrator of New York City's Parks, Recreation and Cultural Affairs Administration complained that the Brooklyn Academy of Music leaked enough to present a water ballet, while Carnegie Hall badly needed interior repairs. The City Center's plumbing leaked and plaster fell on the heads of the performers, and the Lincoln Center plaza was a disgrace.

In an article in the *Saturday Review*, Peter Schrag writes,

> In a nation which denegrates health, transport and public assistance, every citizen is poor. A nation which disregards its poverty is a poor nation. One which watches its public concerns and services fall into decay is hardly a nation at all.

It is a question of priorities. Howard Samuels, then Undersecretary of Commerce, in an address delivered in Hot Springs, Virginia, stated,

> We spend as much for chewing gum as for model cities. We spend as much for hair dye as for grants to urban mass transit. We spend as much for pet food as on food stamps for the poor. We spend more for tobacco than government at all levels spends on higher education. We spend $300 million for jewelry and quarrel over $10,000 for the Teachers' Corps.

Mr. Samuels might also have mentioned that we spend $2 billion on golf courses and $3 billion on pleasure boats.

In his introduction to the twenty-fifth anniversary edition in 1905 of *Progress and Poverty*, Henry George wrote, "Why in a land so bountifully blessed with enough, and more than enough for all, should there be such an inequity of conditions, such heaped wealth interlocked with such deep, debasing want?"

Beyond a doubt, the United States is bountifully blessed with enough and more than enough for all. The gross national product is nearly $1.5 trillion. Personal income is crossing the $1.3 trillion mark. Corporate profits are in excess of $70 billion after taxes. Currency in circulation totals $65 billion while the money supply—checking accounts at banks plus currency in the public hands—averages well over a quarter of a trillion dollars. Time deposits add another $350 billion. The value of the gold stock at Fort Knox exceeds $11.5 billion. The heaped wealth of the nation is estimated as approaching $6 trillion.

Yes, the United States is unbelievably wealthy.

Then where has all the money gone?

We are all familiar with the historic ethos of American life—its myth of frontier classlessness, its spirit of equality. The ancient faith upon which the United States was founded envisioned a seamless, egalitarian society—all men are created equal. Article I, Section 9 of the Constitution proscribes the granting of titles of nobility.

After two hundred years of democracy and independence, it would be difficult for a large majority of Americans to show fewer significant material possessions than if the country had long labored under a grasping, rapacious dictatorship. The economic processes have been so contrived as to strip threadbare most of the populace that once, at least, owned small patches of virgin land. Review the economic history of the United States over the past two centuries. Our material wealth is not the result of seizure from foreign sources. No, it is the result of the wanton subjugation of a previously free people and a previously free economy. It was, in the most literal and true sense, a rape, a conquest of the American nation.

As Karl Marx detailed in *Das Kapital*, this "expropriation of the immediate producers was accomplished with merciless vandalism, under the stimulus of passion the most infamous, the most sordid, the pettiest, the most meanly odious."

The fear of the Jeffersonians that, with great differences of wealth, democracy would end up a meaningless form, more than that, a dangerous fiction, has become a reality. We mouth the old words, the ancient rhetoric of égalité, but we have forgotten the melody. That government of the people, by the people, and for the people has become the feudal fief of the propertied, by the propertied, and for the propertied. Our inheritance, our immense productivity has been pre-empted and parceled out in a kind of domainal system. That beautiful American classlessness has frozen into statuses.

The reality is that American society is based on a class structure that pervades most of the crucial facets of life. The new lords who emerged upon the conquest of the American nation arrayed themselves in the trappings of royalty. Great monarchical palaces and imperial monuments were built. Nor did it take the American language long to recognize the realities of the loss of democracy. There were copper kings, railroad barons, money princes and dukes of Wall Street, and even robber barons—an American aristocracy.

Yes, America now boasts a rich, proud, and privileged order, an aristocracy of wealth, constituting a hierarchy that is as formal and far more powerful than that of the great vassals of the Middle Ages. Britain has her royal family. France has her two hundred families, we have our sixty hereditary families. Their names are household words, Rockefeller, Morgan, Vanderbilt, Field, Whitney, Harriman, Hill, Weyerhauser, Mellon, Woolworth, Goelet, duPont, Ford.

Much of the rest of the American population has been reduced to the status of the lumpen proletariat, "mudsills of society."

It was Theodore Roosevelt who stated, "Of all forms of tyranny, the least attractive and the most vulgar is the tyranny of mere wealth, the tyranny of a plutocracy." Adam Smith talks of the "mean rapacity, the monopolizing spirit of merchants and manufacturers who neither are or ought to be the rulers of mankind." H.L. Mencken writes, "the plutocracy, in a democratic state, tends to take the place of the missing aristocracy, even to be mistaken for it...It lacks all the essential characteristics of a true aristocracy; a clean tradition, culture, public spirit, honesty, honor, courage...It stands under no obligation to the State; it has no public duty."

The discrepancy between what is and what could have been is overwhelming. The promise of America, land of beauty and abundance, land of the free, has somehow been betrayed. How could Americans, ever suspicious of the concentration of political power, have permitted to develop substantially unchallenged such a concentration of economic power as would make a Roman emperor gasp? How could Americans have ignored the clear warning that a free society cannot long coexist with massive concentration of economic power?

Such concentrations of income and wealth make a mockery of political democracy. "One person, one vote" is a sham for the middle class and the poor alike when the rich can, and do, buy political influence.

One recalls the conversation between F. Scott Fitzgerald and Ernest Hemingway. The former remarked, "You know, Ernest, the rich are different from us." To which Hemingway replied, "Yes, I know, they have more money than we do." Of course, the rich are really different from the rest of us because they enjoy that economic freedom, that self-assurance that is characteristic of the possessors of great wealth. Wealth is not subject to old age, illness, or other human frailties. Small wonder that wealth has been termed the only secure power, the only real distinction.

The cold statistics on income and wealth shatter any illusion that economic equalitarianism exists in the United States.

Professor Paul A. Samuelson, Nobel laureate in economics wrote in 1961 in his book, *Economics: An Introductory Analysis*, "If we made an income pyramid out of a child's blocks with each layer portraying $1,000 of income, the peak would be far higher than the Eiffel Tower, but almost all of us would be within a yard of the ground."

A study published in 1972 by Letitia Upton and Nancy Lyons of the Cambridge Institute concludes: "There is a startling and continuing inequality in the distribution of income in the United States and the overall pattern has remained virtually unchanged since World War II." The top one percent of the income pyramid gets more than the bottom twenty percent and the ratio has not changed since 1947. If anything, a study by Peter Henle of the Labor Department detected a persistent trend toward inequality in the distribution of income among wage and salary earners so that from 1958 to 1970 the share earned by the lowest twenty percent of male workers declined to 4.6 percent from 5.1 percent.

In point of fact, A.L. Bowley found that that share of personal income represented by wages has remained relatively steady since 1880 in the United Kingdom and since 1909 in the United States.

Joseph Pechman of the Brookings Institution, in an article entitled *The Rich, The Poor and the Taxes They Pay* appearing in the fall, 1969 issue of *Public Interest,* concluded that the distribution of income in the 1950s may not have been very different from what it was in the early 1920s.

Gabriel Kolko, an outstanding authority on the subject, in his book *Wealth and Power in America*, published in 1962, stated that a radically unequal distribution of income has been characteristic of the American social structure since at least 1910 and that, despite minor year to year fluctuations in the shares of the income tenths, no significant trend toward equality has appeared. From 1910 to 1959, the income of the top ten percent has been consistently larger than that of the entire bottom half.

Mr. Kolko fixed the share of the bottom half of the population at twenty-seven percent of national personal income in 1919 and twenty-three percent in 1959. The Census Bureau reported twenty-two percent for 1968.

Here is one of the great enigmas of American history. Why has the economy stubbornly perpetuated inequality despite progressive income taxation, relatively high employment, widespread educational opportunities, and recurrent wars on poverty?

Inequality is a fact of national life. As in the case of personal income, there is a startling and continuing inequality in the distribution of personal wealth, and the overall pattern has remained virtually unchanged since the founding of the Republic.

Robert Gullman estimated that the top one percent of families in 1810 possessed twenty-one percent of all wealth in the personal sector. Robert J. Lampman, in his famous study that we will discuss in the next chapter, fixed the percentage at an incredible thirty-two percent for 1953, while Dorothy S. Projector and Gertrude S. Weiss set the percentage at thirty-five percent for 1962.

Professor James D. Smith of Pennsylvania State University found that "the degree of concentration (of wealth) did not decrease in the 1960's. If anything, it increased slightly." Inflation and the resulting Giffen Paradox, imposes a particular burden on the poor. This was the conclusion of a research monograph. *Inflation and the Redistribution of Wealth*, written by Professors George L. Bach and James B. Stephenson. The study stated that inflation discriminates most against the poor because they lack political or market power to keep their income rising as fast as prices.

American political rhetoric has consistently condemned inherited wealth as undemocratic and un-American. President Franklin D. Roosevelt, in his tax revision message to Congress on 19 June 1935, stated,

> The transmission from generation to generation of vast fortunes by will, inheritance or gift is not consistent with the ideals and sentiments of the American people. Great accumulation of wealth cannot be justified on the basis of personal or family security. Such inherited economic power is as inconsistent with the ideals of this generation as inherited political power was inconsistent with the ideals of the generation which established our government.

Franklin Roosevelt was echoing the sentiments expressed by many Presidents before him. For instance, Theodore Roosevelt had stated in an earlier tax message,

> No advantage comes either to the country or to the individual inheriting the money by permitting the transmission in their

> entirety of enormous fortunes. . . .The prime object should be to put a constantly increasing burden on the inheritance of these swollen fortunes which it is certainly no benefit to this country to perpetuate.

Herbert Hoover inveighed against the "evils of inherited economic power."

One of the myths of the American scene is the fiction that this nation was dedicated to the removal of the inequities of power and position conferred by law through the accident of birth. Supposedly, there is a maximum degree of concentration of wealth that is tolerable in a democracy and compatible with an ideology of equality of economic opportunity. The inheritance of wealth plays havoc with this ideology. It was Tocqueville, after all, who posed the prospect of an America without classes—an "equality of conditions."

The reality, however, is that the American nation was born to protect wealth and power. A basic distrust and fear of the people was explicit in the attempts of the Founding Fathers to create a self-limiting government. For instance, Charles Pinckney proposed that no one could be President who was not worth at least $100,000 (a vast sum in 1789).

The reality is that inherited wealth plays a significant role in reaching the top of the economic ladder. C. Wright Mills, writing his *The Power Elite* in 1955, estimated that sixty-eight percent of America's great fortunes were inherited rather than self-made. The *Fortune* survey of November 1957, estimated that fifty-five percent of the then-largest fortunes had come into the hands of its current owners by transfer between generations in the form of bequest, gift, insurance proceeds, etc., while forty-five percent was accumulated by the present owners. The Federal Reserve Board found that inherited wealth accounted for a substantial portion of the total assets of fifty-seven percent of those with incomes of over $100,000.

Arthur Lewis, in an article entitled, *America's Centimillionaires*, appearing in the May 1968 *Fortune*, stated that of the sixty-six persons worth over $150 million, over one-half were from clearly recognizable old money families.

The Projector-Weiss study, which we shall also discuss in the next chapter, showed the following ratio of inherited assets per consumer units in 1962:

	WEALTH	
	$100,000 OR MORE	$500,000 OR MORE
Number of Consumer Units	1,200,000	200,000
Inherited Assets		
None	50 percent	39 percent
Small proportion	29	24
Large proportion	20	34

How, in the face of these unquestionable facts, can any informed person argue that the inherited fortune is a thing of the past? One can only chuckle at old Andrew Mellon who sought repeal of the estate tax in the 1920s on the ground that it would be "only two or three generations until private ownership of property would cease to exist." One need only glance through the society pages to realize how the old names still play a dominant role. The Rockefellers, Vanderbilts, Goulds, Belmonts, Whitneys, Mellons, duPonts, Pews, McCormicks, Hearsts, Guggenheims, Lamonts, Huttons, Dukes, Harrimans, Hartfords, Fords, Firestones, and others are still very much with us. Like the names, the money, too, comes from dead men. It was Samuel Butler who wrote, "The money that men make lives after them."

Of all the animals, man alone permits certain of its species to own more treasure, more food, more of everything than he needs to sustain life. There is a magical, inherent quality in this surplus money. Unlike the amoeba that multiplies by dividing, surplus money multiplies by geometric progression. This characteristic of excess money forms the basis for the popular expression: "Them as has, gets." The wellspring of gold that bubbles forth from investment and that multiplies without any expenditure of energy and then is passed on to the heirs has opened huge crevices in the myth of a seamless America.

The concentration of wealth in a tiny number of individuals is rendered even more concentrated by the fact that the big wealth is held mainly in family phalanxes. For instance, included in the list of top wealthholders would be Nelson Rockefeller, Laurance Rockefeller, the late Winthrop Rockefeller, David Rockefeller, and John Rockefeller, 3d. Individually, each would be a power to be reckoned with on the industrial scene. Together, the brothers constitute a formidable force. At the outset of the Congressional hearings on his confirmation as Vice-President, Nelson Rockefeller termed a "myth" the power and influence of his family. Then came the sordid disclosures of his massive gifts and contributions to public servants, including members of the Congress who had to pass judgment on him.

The same situation would hold true for the duPonts, Mellons, Firestones, and many other top wealthholders.

John S. Knight writes,

> The moneybags who constitute less than one per cent of the population of the U.S.A. appropriate two-thirds of the country's national income. The wealth of three clans of multi-billionaires—the Rockefellers, the duPonts and Mellons—exceed one year's wages and the entire savings of all American workers.

6

The Cold Statistics

The distribution of income and wealth in the United States is unbelievably lopsided.

A study conducted by Professors Lester C. Thurow and Robert E.B. Lucas of the Massachusetts Institute of Technology found that from 1947 through 1969, the poorest fifth of American families have received about five percent of total family income and the top fifth about forty-two percent—a ratio of eight to one. The second poorest fifth—the working class—earns only thirteen percent of the total income, while the top five percent have fifteen percent of the income to divide among themselves.

According to the President's 1974 annual Economic Report, these percentages held through 1972. In that year the bottom fifth had 5.1 percent of the nation's income while the top fifth had 41.4 percent. The top five percent enjoyed 15.9 percent. Alice M. Rivlin, budget adviser to the Congress, stated in January 1975 that despite tax and transfer programs and a good deal of rhetoric about eliminating poverty, the United States has been locked into an almost unchanging and uneven income distribution since World War II.

These figures apply to pretax income. After taxes, thanks to all the loopholes, which we will discuss later, these percentages remain almost exactly the same.

The following table, derived from the United States Bureau of the Census, Current Population Reports, gives the share of income received by each fifth of families and by the top ten, five, and one percent for 1968:

FAMILY RANK	INCOME RANGE	PERCENTAGE OF INCOME RECEIVED
Lowest Fifth	Under $4,600	6%
Second Fifth	$4,601 to $7,400	12
Third Fifth	$7,401 to $10,000	18
Fourth Fifth	$10,001 to $13,500	24
Highest Fifth	$13,501 and over	41
Top 10%	$16,000 and over	27
Top 5%	$23,000 and over	14
Top 1%	$42,500 and over	5

These figures show the distribution of income before taxes. A study by the Survey Research Center of the University of Michigan gives the share of income received by each fifth of families and individuals before and after taxes for 1966:

	PERCENTAGE OF AGGREGATE INCOME RECEIVED	
FAMILY RANK	BEFORE TAXES	AFTER TAXES
Lowest Fifth	5%	5%
Second Fifth	11	11
Third Fifth	18	17
Fourth Fifth	23	25
Highest Fifth	43	41

This latter table speaks for itself.

The Bureau of the Census translates the above percentiles into money levels for the 50.5 million American families in 1968:

INCOME LEVEL	NUMBER OF FAMILIES	PERCENTAGE	
		FAMILIES	INCOME
All Families	50.5 million	100%	100%
Under $3,000	5.2 million	10	2
$3,001 to $7,000	13.4 million	27	14
$7,001 to $10,000	11.8 million	23	20
$10,001 to $15,000	12.6 million	25	31
$15,001 to $25,000	6.1 million	12	23
$25,001 to $59,000	1.2 million	2	7
$50,001 and over	150,000	0.3	2
Median income	$8,600		
Mean income	$9,700		

Roughly fifteen percent of the families receive about one-third of the total income, while the remaining eighty-five percent share the remaining two-thirds of the income.

We rattle merrily along setting down income statistics as if we really knew what we were doing. Actually, we do not have a sure-fire definition of income. Tax expert Benjamin Okner of the Brookings Institution states, "It's amazing that in the richest country in the world, where we spend money collecting all sorts of obscure statistics, we can't find out what total family incomes really are."

For instance, it is the feeling of Gabriel Kolko that the uncomputed income of the upper class, that is, deferred compensation, pension plans, stock options, consumption expenditures through expense accounts, profit sharing, etc., would raise disposable income for this group two to three percentage points.

Here, we are defining income in the usual, narrower tax-law way. But for our broad purposes, it will suffice to illustrate our message—that income distributions in the United States are woefully skewed.

A study directed by Simon Kuznetz, another Nobel laureate in economics, for the National Bureau of Economic

Research in 1953, determined that property income (rent, interest, and dividends) make up 15.8 percent of the total income received by the entire population, but 48.7 percent of the income of the top 1 percent. The top 1 percent received 40 percent of the national total of property income. Norman G. Kurland, the executive director of the Study of Economic Systems, found that less than one of every one hundred households receives significant income from capital.

Since to have capital gains one must own property, it is not surprising that only one taxpayer in twelve is able to report such gains and that three-quarters of capital gains are enjoyed by the wealthiest two percent of Americans. The same two percent received seventy-four percent of all dividends in 1966.

Income is who *gets* what; wealth is who *has* what.

Since incomes fluctuate from year to year, the amount received during any particular twelve-month period provides a less-certain basis for identifying the rich. Wealth provides a much more stable measure because it represents an accumulation over many years and is less likely to fluctuate than income. The point is that a high income is not necessarily a measure of individual wealth.

If, in the richest country in the world, where we spend money collecting all sorts of obscure statistics, we cannot find out what total family incomes really are, imagine our dilemma when we turn to statistics of personal wealth. Such figures are practically nonexistent. Even the Statistical Abstract of the United States, that mine of information, which devotes table after table to income statistics, sets aside only two pages of indifferent importance, in its 1974 edition, to personal wealth.

In the preface to his classic pioneer text on the subject, *The Share of Top Wealth Holders in National Wealth, 1922 to 1956,* published by the Princeton University Press in 1962 for the National Bureau of Economic Research, Robert J. Lampman wrote, "Relatively little inquiry has been made into the size distribution of wealth in the United States. Hence, this study becomes part of a scant literature on the subject of personal wealth holding." To this date, strange as it may seem, there are no official comprehensive estimates of the national wealth.

The lack of systematic empirical investigation of this subject in the United States is certainly not due to a lack of interest in the facts of wealth distribution or an unconcern with the questions that revolve around these vital facts. The public has shown its fascination with the fabulously rich by grasping up everything written on the subject.

The cause for the paucity of written material about the wealthy is not difficult to explain. The rich are probably the most inaccesible people in the country to the researchers. They do not call on the facilities of public agencies where statistics can be gathered and correlated as the poor are forced to do. Read the memoirs of some of our wealthiest citizens. You will find them, on the whole, to be extremely nervous and very much on the defensive. They are alert as any criminal under arrest to the traditional warning that anything they say may be used against them.

Ask any man, no matter how wealthy, "Are you rich?" and he will snap back "It's none of your damn business." Wealth is private, sacrosanct, inviolate, and its investigation is repugnant to the ideals of Western political systems. "God gave me my money," proclaimed John D. Rockefeller.

Professor Lampman of the University of Wisconsin used as a springboard for his basic work the requirement that inheritance tax returns be filed with the Internal Revenue Service for estates with assets of $60,000 or more. His transformation, in 286 pages with 138 formidable tables and 37 charts, of the recorded evidence on decedents in a given year into a distribution of wealth among persons who were alive in that year has been compared with the work of an archeologist who reconstructs the artifacts of an earlier civilization from buried or scattered ruins.

Terming those who possessed a net worth in excess of $60,000 "top wealthholders," Lampman placed 1,659,000 persons in that category in 1953. They comprised 1.04 percent of all persons, 1.6 percent of the adult population, 2.28 percent of spending units, and 2.35 percent of married couples. Their median age was fifty-four and they possessed 32 percent of all wealth in the personal sector. They held 82.2 percent of all corporate stock outstanding, 100 percent of state and municipal bonds, 38.2 percent of federal bonds, 88.5 percent of other bonds, 29.1 percent of the cash, 36.2 percent of mortgages and notes, 13.3 percent of life insurance reserves and 16.1 percent of real estate. One-half of one percent of the population owned 25 percent of the wealth.

The personally owned wealth of the total population in 1953 was fixed at $1.04 trillion, giving an average gross net worth for all 103 million adults of slightly less than $10,000. For the top wealthholders, the average was $182,000; for the bottom half of the population, the average was $1,800.

A parallel survey of consumer finances conducted by the University of Michigan for the Federal Reserve Board in the same year determined that the eleven percent of spending units with a net worth of $25,000 or more held fifty-six percent of total assets and sixty percent of total net worth. While this group held only thirty percent of consumer capital, they held eighty percent of business and investment assets.

A Federal Reserve Board study, conducted by Dorothy S. Projector and Gertrude S. Weiss in 1962, found that 59.8 percent of the population owned wealth of under $10,000, while only 0.4 percent held wealth in excess of $500,000. This is in line with the Upton-Lyons findings for the Cambridge Institute that the top fifth of Americans, ranked by wealth, owned 77 percent of personal wealth in 1962—three times more than the entire wealth of the bottom 80 percent.

The Projector-Weiss survey sets forth the distribution of wealth on 31 December 1962:

	CONSUMER UNITS		PERCENT OF TOTAL
WEALTH	IN MILLIONS	PERCENT	WEALTH
Total	57.9	100	100
Negative	1.0	2	—
Zero	4.7	8	—
$1-$999	9.0	16	—
$1,000-$4,999	10.8	19	2
$5,000-$9,999	9.1	16	5
$10,000-$24,999	13.3	23	18
$25,000-$49,999	6.2	11	18
$50,000-$99,999	2.5	4	14
$100,000-$199,999	0.7	1	8
$200,000-$499,999	0.5	1	13
$500,000 and over	0.2	—	22

These figures tally very closely with those of the Thurow-Lucas survey cited earlier. They found that, for 1969, the top 20 percent of consumer units held 77 percent of all wealth. 2.5 percent of all families accounted for 44 percent of all private assets. 25 percent of the families had no net worth to report.

The Urban Institute estimated that, in 1969, the 4.4 percent of the super-rich of the population owned 35.6 percent of consumer wealth, including 63 percent of privately held corporate stock, 78 percent of state and local bonds, 74 percent of Federal obligations and almost all corporate and foreign bonds and notes. Their net worth averaged $200,000.

A study by the Wharton School, published in the November 1974 issue of the Commerce Department Survey of Current Business found the richest two-tenths of one percent of Americans, with incomes in excess of $100,000, owning 30.2 percent of all corporate stock in 1971. The top one percent had incomes in excess of $50,000 and owned 51.1 percent of all the stock while the top 10 percent owned 74 percent.

It should be noted that, in 1969, nearly one-half of all American families had less than $500 in savings, while one-fifth had none. Less than one-third had more than $2,000 in liquid assets. The University of Michigan Survey Research Center determined median liquid asset holdings for all families in 1971 to be $700.

If we turn to the other end of the spectrum and consider millionaires as a separate category, we find that they comprise 2/10 of 1 percent of the population and own 7 percent of all privately held wealth and 21 percent of all corporate stock.

The Internal Revenue Service tabulated the number of millionaires in 1962:

WEALTH IN MILLIONS	NUMBER OF MILLIONAIRES
$1- $2	43,690
2- 3	10,417
3- 5	7,211
5- 10	4,277
10 and over	1,847
Total	67,442

James D. Smith and Staunton K. Calvert of the Statistics Division of the Internal Revenue Service estimated the sources of wealth of millionaires for 1958.

SOURCE	AMOUNT IN BILLIONS	PERCENTAGE	PERCENTAGE OF TOTAL UNITED STATES WEALTH
Total	$108.2	100%	7%
Real estate	9.2	9	2
Federal bonds	2.1	2	3
State and local bonds	6.6	6	42
Other bonds	0.7	1	14
Corporate stock	54.5	50	21
Cash	3.8	3	18
Notes and mortgages	2.7	2	6
Life insurance equity	0.6	1	6
Miscellaneous	28.0	26	10

Arthur M. Lewis, in his famous study published in *Fortune* in 1968, listed 153 persons in the United States with net worths of more than $100 million each.

Here, the reader should heed the caution of George Katone and John B. Lansing that the findings of even the best studies tend to seriously underestimate the amount of wealth held by the super-rich.

The Smith-Calvert study, in extending the Lampman findings to 1958, declared that the "data supported Lampman's conclusion that the share of the top wealthholders has been increasing since 1949."

When the *Wall Street Journal* reported the above-mentioned Urban Institute study of taxpayers worth $60,000 or more, labeling them "super-rich," many readers wrote in asking whether the $60,000 was a misprint. The publication explained, "No, it wasn't...The fact is that wealth is surprisingly concentrated."

In the same way that income taxes failed to affect the lopsided distribution of income, inheritance taxes have failed to affect the lopsided distribution of wealth. Estate taxes have failed, if it ever was their intent, to break down the artificial barriers to class mobility. Only four percent of the estates of adults who die in any one year are required to file inheritance taxes, and only twenty-five percent of the total wealth of these decedents is subject to tax.

7

Where Has All the Power Gone?

The lords, barons, princes, and dukes of our new nobility of wealth - where do they exercise their suzerainty? Where are their kingdoms, baronies, dukedoms, provinces, fiefs? From what castles, over what moats, flying what banners, do they sally forth to do battle for God and country? Who are their retainers, serfs, vassals?

The medieval panoply of feudalism has been duplicated in the corporate organization of American life. The seat of power has moved from the royal courts to the board rooms of the executive suites of the giant corporations. Antony Jay shrewdly recognized this similitude in his book, *Machiavelli and Management*.

We have mentioned before the gilded names of Rockefeller, duPont, Ford, etc., in connection with the American aristocracy and as leaders of society. Their preeminence, their status, their position stems from their control of designated corporations, which control, as we mentioned earlier, is held by family phalanxes. For instance, the family name Rockefeller is synonymous with Standard Oil, duPont with duPont, Ford with Ford.

Pew can be identified with Sun Oil, Mellon with Gulf Oil, Firestone with Firestone Tire, Hartford with A&P, Eastman with Eastman Kodak, Haughton with Corning Glass, Dorrance with Campbell Soup, Olin with Olin Mathieson, Post with General Foods, Rosenwald with Sears Roebuck, McCormick with International Harvester, Harkness with Standard Oil, Duke with Liggett-Myers Tobacco, Pitcairn with Pittsburgh Plate Glass, Clark with Singer, Reynolds with R.J. Reynolds Tobacco, Kress with S.H. Kress, Deere with Deere, Field with Marshall Field, Weyerhauser with Weyerhauser, Hanna with National Steel, Crane with Crane, Watson with IBM, Colgate with Colgate, Avery with U.S. Gypsum, Hutton with Woolworth, Heinz with H.J. Heinz, Bronfman with Seagram, Wrigley with Wrigley, Keck with Superior Oil, Lilly with Eli Lilly, Busch with Anheuser-Busch, Kaiser with Kaiser Industries, Sarnoff with RCA, Rockwell with Rockwell International, Harriman with Union Pacific, Guggenheim with Kennecott Copper, Dow with Dow Chemical, Widener with American Tobacco, Biddle with American Cyanamid, Milbank with CPC, Astor with Western Union, Kleberg with the King Ranch, and so on.

Each of these corporations holds one distinction in common. Each occupies a prominent position duly certified and sealed on the social register list of *Fortune's* five hundred largest corporations, the Debrett's peerage of American business.

It comes as a shock to realize how incredibly small a handful of individuals in how incredibly small a handful of companies commands America's economic resources making life and death decisions that affect our very lives.

The top ten corporations on *Fortune's* list of the largest industrial firms had sales of $100 billion in 1968, employed over two million people and enjoyed profits in excess of $5 billion. Seven companies (General Motors, Ford, American Telephone and Telegraph, Exxon, Texaco, Gulf Oil, and IBM) earned twenty-five percent of all business profits in 1964.

Studies conducted in 1969 by the staff of the Cabinet Committee on Price Stability found that the twenty, fifty, one hundred, and two hundred largest industrial firms controlled the following percentage of total assets of all corporations:

CORPORATE SIZE GROUP	PERCENT OF TOTAL ASSETS 1950	1965
20 largest	14.5%	18.0%
50 largest	30.2	35.2
100 largest	38.6	45.4
200 largest	46.7	55.4

Dr. Willard Mueller, chief of the Bureau of Economics at the Federal Trade Commission, testified before the Senate Committee on Small Business on 15 March 1967 that the two hundred largest industrial companies then owned two-thirds of all manufacturing assets. At that time, the top two hundred firms held the same share of the total assets as the one thousand largest had owned in 1941. The one hundred largest held a greater share of all manufacturing assets than the two hundred largest in 1950.

A Federal Trade Commission report for 1958 showed that the top one hundred corporations accounted for 50 percent of manufacturing profits and the top 200 for 62.8 percent. The 87 corporations with assets of $1 billion or more in 1969 had increased their share of total corporate assets from 26 percent to 46 percent since 1959. Although the number of corporations with assets under $1 billion had increased by 44,000 in the decade, their share of the total assets fell from 74 percent to 54 percent. The share of corporate profits falling to the giant eighty-seven companies made up 49 percent of manufacturing profits and was equal to that of all other 195,000 manufacturing firms put together. For example, of the 32,000 food manufacturers in the nation, 71 percent of the industry's profits were made by about one hundred companies, while the fifty largest companies account for nearly sixty percent of the total food manufacturing assets.

Of the 1,542,000 active corporations reporting in 1968, the 274,000 companies with annual receipts of $500,000 or more, representing 17.8 percent of the total, accounted for 91.4 percent of all receipts. For 1969, the three-tenths of one percent of all employers reporting under Social Security who employed over five hundred employees accounted for 27.5 percent of all persons gainfully employed. The 2.2 percent with one hundred or more employees employed 50.6 percent of all persons holding jobs.

The United States Department of Commerce's *Annual Survey of Manufacturers* for 1970 gives the share of total value added by manufacture by the largest companies:

COMPANY RANK GROUP	PERCENT OF VALUE ADDED BY MANUFACTURE
Largest 50 companies	24
Largest 100 companies	33
Largest 150 companies	38
Largest 200 companies	43

If anything, these figures probably understate the importance of the largest corporations because of intercorporate holdings. Relationships among the largest corporations are extremely difficult to untangle because of the problem of identifying nonconsolidated holdings. Between 1960 and 1968, for example, the top two hundred corporations set up at least 705 jointly owned subsidiaries with other corporations; one-fifth of them with other members of the top two hundred. In 1965, the top fifty firms shared 520 interlocking directorships with other corporations in the top one thousand. In 1962, the twenty-nine largest manufacturing companies shared interlocking directorships with 745 industrial and commercial corporations, 330 banks and fifty-one other corporations. In 1967, forty-nine banks held interlocking directorships with 6,591 companies.

When we realize the strength of any one of these giant corporations, the significance of these statistics dazzles the imagination. Take General Motors with assets of over $20 billion and 800,000 employees, until recently the number one corporation both in the United States and in the world, which boasts a budget that is larger than that of any of the fifty states and of every nation on earth with the exception of the United States and the Soviet Union. Without giving consideration to its other product lines from locomotives to refrigerators, the fact that General Motors controls 51.7 percent of the domestic passenger car market should cause one to sit up and take notice. She, together with Ford and Chrysler, control 96.6 percent of the total market.

Xerox holds more than fifty percent of the photo copy market. American Telephone and Telegraph's Bell System barely tolerates the approximately two thousand independent companies. The forty-two billion annual gross income of Exxon, the number one corporation, exceeds the gross national product of Denmark; IBM that of Portugal. No less than seventy-three percent of the computers in domestic use bear the label IBM. That behemoth had sales of $12 billion in 1974 and profits of $1.8 billion. It, together with Honeywell and Sperry Rand's Univac, account for eighty-five percent of all computers sold. U.S. Steel accounts for twenty-five percent of national raw steel output and together with the three next largest for fifty-four percent. Kellogg, General Mills, and General Foods, between them, control eighty-two percent of the prepared food market.

General Electric, Westinghouse, and General Telephone and Electronics dominate the electric lamp industry; Goodyear, Firestone, and Uniroyal the tire business: Pittsburgh Plate Glass and Libbey-Owens-Ford the manufacture of flat glass; American Can and Continental Can the making of metal containers; duPont and Hercules the making of explosives; Texas Gulf and Freeport the extraction of sulphur; Hertz, the number-two Avis, and National the auto rental industry; Proctor and Gamble, Lever Bros., and Colgate-

Palmolive the manufacture of soap and detergents; NBC, CBS, and ABC the television networks: These are oligopolies.

Nor is this concentration limited to industrial firms. Of the fourteen thousand commercial banks in the United States, one hundred control fifty percent of all deposits. The ten largest life insurance companies have written 56.9 percent of the life insurance in force and hold 61.8 percent of all assets. The ten largest fire and casualty companies account for 19.6 percent of all industry assets. Even in the case of charitable foundations, less than seven percent of their numbers hold over ninety percent of the more than $25 billion in assets. Thus, even philanthropy is concentrated in the hands of the wealthy few.

Attorney General John N. Mitchell, warned in 1969,

> The danger that this super-concentration poses to our economic, political and social structure cannot be overestimated. . .This leaves us with the unacceptable probability that the nation's manufacturing and financial assets will continue to be concentrated in the hands of fewer and fewer people.

In that year, 1969, 4,550 concerns ceased to exist. The following number of mergers of large manufacturing and mining companies occurred in the following periods:

PERIOD	NUMBER OF MERGERS
1920-1924	2,235
1925-1929	4,583
1930-1934	1,687
1935-1939	577
1940-1944	906
1945-1949	1,505
1950-1954	1,424
1955-1959	3,365
1960-1964	4,366
1965-1969	8,213
1970	1,351
1971	1,011

In their book, *The Modern Corporation and Private Property,* Adolf A. Berle and Gardiner C. Means determined that of the top two hundred firms in 1929, 154 had been so listed in 1919. Only twenty-one had been outside the magic circle a decade earlier, while twenty-three had been merged with others in the top two hundred, and two liquidated. Of the top twenty firms in 1960, only four had not been in the top fifty in 1919. Of these, General Telephone and Electronics had previously been listed as an utility and IBM had been number fifty-five.

We find few, if any, cases of new corporations roaring up to the summit because of inventions or internal competitive growth. Between 1948 and 1968 the top two hundred firms acquired assets in excess of $50 billion through mergers. If we compare *Fortune's* 1969 list of the top five hundred with the 1971 roster, we will find that thirty-one companies had been displaced. Of these, twenty-six were acquired by corporations already on the list, while the remaining five had been in the bottom thirty positions.

One Wall Street commentator stated,

> A good merger is like marrying a rich woman and taking her money. It's as sweet as that, sweeter even, because you can have as many of these brides as you want and you don't have to live with them any longer than you want to. . .Best of all, you do it with borrowed money. Never use your own.

The character of business mergers has changed. In the period 1926 to 1930, seventy-six percent of all recorded mergers were of the horizontal type, and five percent were vertical. By contrast, in the period of merger heyday from 1966 to 1969, horizontal mergers made up nine percent of the total, the vertical 10 percent, and conglomerate mergers accounted for the difference.

The House of Representatives Antitrust Subcommittee's report entitled, "Investigation of Conglomerate Corporations," issued in June 1971, determined that, "combination frequently had an injurious affect on efficiency, on production and on corporate values." Five separate economic studies (by Reid, Kelly, Fogarty, Eslick, and Arnold) have all concluded that there was no relationship between conglomeration and efficiency. The Cabinet Committee on Price Stabilization concluded that the merger boom was "not rooted in technological imperatives."

The AFL-CIO has warned that "the urge to merge" among America's giant corporations carried the danger of eventually turning the nation into one enormous company-owned store. Justice Louis Brandeis called it "unsatiated aggrandizement". . ."the curse of bigness."

Growth is the *sine qua non* of capitalism. As firms saturate their local markets, they broaden their horizons and seek new markets. Here again, the giant corporations monopolized the new markets. Ninety-three corporations accounted for fifty percent of all United States exports in 1966. It soon became apparent to the great corporations that, instead of expanding existing plants to supply these new markets, it was often more economical to open new factories near the foreign markets and to employ labor and purchase raw materials in the area.

Thus was born the multinational corporation. The emergence of massive transnational companies began a century ago when Singer Sewing Machines set up its first foreign factory. By 1914, General Electric, Ford, and others had expanded to other lands. However, the movement overseas did not begin on a broad front until the late 1940s. It was led by American corporations that saw lucrative new markets in countries rebuilding their war-torn economies, as well as opportunities to produce cheaply abroad for sale at home.

As the great combines extended their tentacles beyond the national boundaries, American overseas direct investment increased from $11.8 billion in 1950, to $32 billion in 1960, to $86 billion in 1971. Two-thirds of this postwar growth was in Western Europe, and most of that was concentrated in such fast growing nonextractive industries as chemicals, electronics, autos and computers. The number of foreign subsidiaries of United States firms increased from 2,300 in 1950 to more than 8,000 in 1970, while total foreign assets controlled reached $125 billion and annual production amounted to $156 billion.

There are 298 giant United States-based corporations regarded as multinational, while some 3,600 additional American firms have at least one foreign subsidiary.

The quintessential multinational conglomerate is, of course, the sovereign state of ITT. Once the low profile manager of telephone exchanges in Latin American republics, ITT is now selling everything from ham to hotel rooms, to insurance, to books, to homes, to auto rentals. The parent company encompasses one thousand firms in seventy nations with 428,000 employees, annual revenues of $11 billion, and profits of nearly half a billion dollars.

Seven American oil companies control three-quarters of world oil markets outside North America and the Communist bloc. IBM, Honeywell and other United States-based computer-makers control eighty percent of the European market.

J.J. Servan-Schreiber, in his 1967 book *The American Challenge*, warned of an impending takeover of the European economy by American-based multinationals. M. Servan-Schreiber noted that United States multinationals abroad amount to the third largest economy in the world, outranked only by the domestic United States economy and the Soviet Union. Today the United States; tomorrow the world!

How, in the face of these indisputable facts, can any informed person cling to the fantasy of the sturdy, independent, competitive, small entrepreneur? The folklore of the Western farmer, the small shopkeeper, the Yankee trader, the inventor artisan in his garage are dreams. Myths die hard. No, Virginia, it is not necessarily so that profits are good for the poor; or that hard work can still make you rich; or that the poor are that way because they are lazy; or that you can create economic equality by spending more on education; or that widespread stock ownership has created a people's capitalism in America; or that antitrust laws are a barrier to excessive concentrations of wealth. It has been said, Virginia, that the reality of Big Business in America is like sex in Victorian England—our big, dirty secret.

We look back to Adam Smith's ideal of the small entrepreneur whose selfishness could be made to serve the public interest by the "invisible hand" of competition. Smith advocated that corporate enterprise be limited to banking, insurance, canals, and waterworks—activities requiring large amount of capital capable of being amassed only by corporations—because he foresaw that corporations in other fields would grow powerful enough to break free from the grip of the "invisible hand." Technological advances, however, necessitated huge aggregations of capital in other industries, leading to widespread creation of corporations. They grew in size and power to dimensions undreamed of by Smith. Gardiner Means stated that the modern corporation has undermined classical economic theory as effectively as the quantum undermined classical physics at the beginning of the twentieth-century.

It would have been beyond Smith's imagination to conceive that someday the citizen would be born in a hospital organized as a corporate body; fed his first bottle of milk supplied by a corporation; clothed in diapers fashioned by another corporation; taken in a corporation-built automobile to a corporation-built home; furnished by another assortment of corporations. He grows to adulthood and goes to work for a corporation and becomes a customer of many corporations. Ultimately, he is buried in a corporate-made coffin. The corporation dominates our lives from the first breath of life to the last. Corporate economic power is the dominant reality in the American economy.

As the corporations waxed larger and larger, the industrial system evolved into a penumbra of the state. Hobbes termed the corporation "a chip-off-the-block of sovereignty." The line between industry and the state became increasingly artificial and indistinct. A.A. Berle tells us that we must come to think of the major corporations in somewhat the same terms as heretofore applied to the nation-states.

John Kenneth Galbraith stated that men will someday look back in amusement at the pretense that once caused people to refer to General Electric, duPont, or Vickers as private business. Does it really matter that the postal service is a public corporation and the telephone is a private one when both are deteriorating and increasingly expensive. Ferdinand Lundberg terms the giant corporations "Finpolities" and describes them as more like governments or governmental departments.

Almost a century before Calvin Coolidge proclaimed, "The business of America is business," Thomas Low Nichols, a social critic, wrote, "The real work of America is to make money for the sake of making it. It is an end and not a means." Nichols described "the universal and everlasting struggle for wealth," which was recognized as "the only secure power, the only real distinction."

Henry Luce had correctly gauged the pulse of the nation when he founded *Fortune* magazine in 1929 to exemplify the thesis that

> business is obviously the greatest single denominator of interest among the active leading citizens of the United States of America . . .the distinctive expression of the American genius.

With his usual insight, Albert Einstein had sensed the canonization of business in this country. He wrote from Princeton in 1938: "In general, there is little appreciation for the finer things, especially because the businessman is the national saint." President Coolidge had once remarked that "the man who builds a factory builds a temple, the man who works there worships there."

Professor Galbraith traces the evolution of power from medieval times. During the feudal ages, land was scarce, labor abundant, and little capital investment required—thus power rested with the landlords. With the birth of the industrial revolution—labor still being relatively abundant and land superfluous—power moved to those who controlled the supply of capital—the bankers. Once assured of capital, the entrepreneurs, the managers of industry took over. As business concentration ran its course and consolidated control into a few monopolies and oligopolies, the technostructure of the modern corporation had emerged.

Money is power. Money means political clout. The substance of A.A. Berle's book, *Power*, is that property and power are essentially the same substance. Economics is a branch of government. Once demystified, the dismal science is nothing less than the study of power. Inexorably, over any substantial period of time, economic power translates into political power. Corporate monopoly is not just another interest group in American life, it is the keystone of power. Those who own the wealth of a nation soon own its government, too. Thorstein Veblen concluded, "The American national establishment is a government of business men for business ends." The subordination of politics to economics, has been called the greatest sin of the past century.

Morton Mintz and Jerry S. Cohen ask, "Who owns and operates the United States?" They answer, "Big business is government." Woodrow Wilson had stated,

> The masters of the government of the United States are the combined capitalists and manufacturers of the United States. . . The government of the United States at present is a foster child of the special interests.

It was Karl Marx who explained how the government acted as the executive committee of the ruling class. For politics may be defined as the organization of power. Or, as the acerbic Ambrose Bierce put it, "Politics is the conduct of public affairs for private advantage." The laws then will reflect the power structure. Laws require coercion for enforcement. Power, law, and coercion are the basic stuff of politics.

We see in the United States of America one of the best examples in history of a genuine timocracy. The governmental system is dedicated to the promotion of personal wealth and the protection of large fortunes. The workings of the capitalist state were best exemplified by the draft that routinely confiscated lives to fight wars but dared not confiscate money or property. These it held more inviolate than life—which therefore must be borrowed and repaid with interest. Thus, President Truman's seizure of the steel industry in 1952 was invalidated by the Supreme Court.

Where once the state was the private property of the prince, today America is the private property of a small wealthy clique. We see here the incarnation of the German and Japanese Zaibatsu—the great controlling family industrial combines. To paraphrase Karl Marx's comments on the July monarchy, the United States government emerges as nothing other than a joint stock company for the exploitation of America's national wealth.

Administrations may come and administrations may go. Political parties may gain and political parties may relinquish control. But the permanent government of oil, steel, banking, and munitions never goes out of office.

The political capital of the United States may be in Washington, but for those who recognize money as more formidable than laws, the real power is elsewhere—in Detroit, in New York. In these latter cities we may dimly discern the outline of a permanently concentrated group of officials, holding a paramount and virtually unchallenged power position over the American industrial economy. In these latter cities are the true locations of power, immense, anonymous, impregnable, immovably embedded in society. The great authority exercised there is socially irresponsible and unresponsive, locked beyond the reach of the democratic process. "I owe the people nothing," said J.P. Morgan. We have responded to the charge that government was the kept woman of business by wedding Wall Street to Washington.

The bureaucracy—government and business interlocked and indistinguishable, opposite sides of the same coin—merely implements, although with brutal force where necessary, the prescribed script. The individual bureaucrats play a game of musical chairs between government and business.

The military-industrial complex against which Dwight Eisenhower warned the nation has become the military-industrial-executive department complex. Gordon W. Rule thinks the old general must be twitching in his grave. Generals, businessmen, and bureaucrats now act in interchangeable roles to the point of blurring the dividing line between their real roles. Northrop had employed seven high-ranking United States military officers, including four-star generals, during the time that that company was accused of secret illegal political contributions. A September 1975 study showed that 350 top-level regulatory Federal officials once worked for the industry they now regulate.

In the corridors of power, money talks in its husky, silky voice of cash, power, and celebrity. John W. Gardner writes,

> It isn't a pleasant thing to admit that in this great nation elective offices can be purchased; that votes of Federal, state and local officials are bought and sold every day; that access of the people to their government is blocked by a Chinese wall of money. It isn't pleasant but it's a fact—and, today, a dangerous fact.

Mr. Gardner goes on to state that the access of money to power is blocking the access of people to power, and that the pervasive and degrading influence of money in politics is making it very difficult for the honest politician to be effective. The money changers have *not* fled from their high seats in the temple of our civilization. They have appropriated them.

Thirteen corporations, including Gulf Oil, Northrop, American Airlines, and 3M have pleaded guilty to making illegal campaign contributions. Millions of dollars were set aside in secret slush funds.

We find that we take for granted the wealth qualifications for the aspiring politician. From Colonial times, the rich and the well-born traditionally have held the reins of power, for they alone could afford to take the time from their own affairs to concern themselves with public matters. C. Wright Mills, in *The American Political Elite: A Collective Portrait,* analyzed the economic backgrounds of 495 men who held high office between 1789 and 1950. He found that fifty-eight percent of them were from the top five to ten percent of economic standing in the population.

A survey conducted by the Associated Press in April 1968 found that at least one out of every five United States senators is considered to be a millionaire. Compare this ratio with the percentage of millionaires to the total population cited earlier in this book. No wonder the Senate bears the reputation of being the nation's most exclusive club.

As a case study, let us turn to the two-volume report on E.I. duPont De Nemours Co. of Delaware, entitled *The Company State*, which was published in November 1971 by a group of young investigators, mostly students, working under Ralph Nader. The report begins by acknowledging that the company "has a national reputation as a liberal, progressive firm."

It then goes on to demonstrate how duPont exercises "squirearchical" domination of government, politics, taxing policy, welfare, education, urban planning, public transportation, and public information in Delaware. A section on government details the company's grip on public office. "Officials from the governor to the state Attorney General to the United States senators and representatives are identified as family members or persons" entrenched in the corporate establishment. To quote the report, "In Delaware, the duPont Company and its owners, the duPont family, are so powerful that there is no line between corporation and government."

The study concluded that while dominating "virtually every major aspect of Delaware life," the giant chemical concern pursued its narrow corporate interests rather than the public good. Further, by maintaining "a virtual monopoly" over the news through its control of the state's two largest newspapers, *The Morning News* and *The Evening Journal* in Wilmington, duPont has insulated itself from public criticism.

Charles B. McCoy, the company's president and chairman, replied,

> The report expresses a political philosophy that is alien to the essential directions of American public policy and proposes to alter drastically our economic system, which is based on free enterprise.

We shall have a few words to say about free enterprise in the next chapter.

As another case study, consider the report entitled *The Paper Plantation* written by William C. Osborn of the Ralph Nader Center for the Study of Responsive Law. The report charged that the pulp and paper industry in Maine has imposed "a one-crop economy with a one-crop politics which exploits the water, air, soil and people of a beautiful state." The industry has become a law onto themselves, deciding what laws to enact, what laws they should disregard, what laws they should perforate with comfortable loopholes, how much taxes they should pay, who would get elected or stay elected—in short, they were and continue to be private government without accountabilities.

Jack Newfield and Jeff Greenfield, in *A Populist Manifesto: The Making of a New Majority*, pose the fundamental question of politics which question bears repeating, "Who holds power and by what right?"

8

The Welfare State: Welfare for Whom?

We have all heard the United States referred to as a welfare state. For whose welfare does this welfare state operate? Certainly, not for the benefit of the poor.

The late Senator Robert F. Kennedy, back in 1967, had described the present system of aiding the poor as a "system of handouts, a second rate set of social services, which damages and demeans its recipients," and destroys "any semblance of human dignity." He continued,

> We have created a welfare system which aids only a fourth of those who are poor, which forces men to leave their families so that public assistance can be obtained, which has created a dependence on their fellow citizens that is degrading and distasteful to giver and receiver alike.

Frances Fox Piven and Richard A. Cloward's book, *Regulating The Poor* is a must if one would understand the workings of the public welfare system. The size of the welfare rolls and the amounts of benefits are political decisions based on political considerations and not on considerations of need.

Relief-giving arises from the need to counter disorders during periods of mass unemployment and to enforce low wages during periods of economic and political stability. Thus, the mechanism of welfare is best understood not as charity but, as Piven and Cloward explain, as a system for regulating the poor. Relief-giving expands only when the destitute become clamorous and disorderly on a scale that threatens the political stability. Thus, only when black discontent finally erupted in mass protests, riots, and crime in the 1960s did the relief rolls finally erupt as well.

Welfare payments are blackmail paid to soothe the turbulent waves of protest. Once the turbulence subsides, the relief system shifts from moderating disorder to regulating labor. The able-bodied poor are forced off the welfare rolls and into the low-wage labor pool. A few of the aged, the disabled, and others who are of no value as workers are left on the rolls to be demeaned and degraded. The remaining unfortunate recipients are caricatured into a pariah class whose shame serves to exalt, by contrast, the meanest labor at the meanest wage—at the same time, instilling in the able-bodied a fear and loathing of the dole.

Let us put into its proper perspective this so-called welfare state. Aid to the poor has always been most niggardly. Even the war on poverty, which was more of a truce than a war, never absorbed more than a little over two percent of the resources spent on real war and military preparations in any one year. The war on poverty never presumed to contest the woefully unequal distribution of wealth and income in the United States. At most, it sought to come to grips only with the unequal access to the lowest paying jobs.

The principal beneficiaries of the war on poverty were not the poor but the bureaucrats who supposedly ministered to them. Giant corporations, like ITT, Litton, and RCA who won the fat antipoverty contracts, reaped the harvest; the poor were left the crumbs.

Thus has it always been. Like it or not, the relief program is a feeding trough for the institutionalized sanctimonious welfare industry—a monster exploiting human suffering. All it does is tacitly condone social injustice and keep conditions as they are—help to keep poor people poor.

Daniel P. Moynihan, in his book *The Politics of Guaranteed Income,* blames the scuttling of President Nixon's Family Assistance Plan upon the patrons of the poor who are now enriched—politically, professionally, and financially—by the services strategy of providing indirect aid to the poor.

If the welfare state is not run for the benefit of the poor, then for whose benefit does it operate? The answer is only too self-evident: the welfare state operates for the welfare of the rich—the individual rich and corporate rich.

The working of the United States welfare state is controlled lock, stock, and barrel by the naked power unveiled in the previous chapter.

Money begets power and power begets money. We have isolated the sources of power in the United States. To what ends is this power exercised? How is it made manifest? Yes, money is power: money means political clout. Inexorably, economic power translates into political power. Political power translates into government contracts, subsidies, tariffs, quotas, monopolies, tax loopholes, bail-outs, government loans, handouts, antitrust immunity.

The government of the United States functions like it is designed by those with power to serve those with power. The institutions of the nation are structured to serve the interests of the economic royalists. In practice, the free enterprise system means rugged individualism for the poor and socialism for the rich.

The government and its institutions turn their backs in stark indifference on the people not rich enough to make campaign contributions, not educated enough to demand higher wages and better jobs, not white enough to ever become either rich or well educated. Contrast the reception accorded to the 1968 Poor People's Campaign in Washington's Resurrection City to the welcome mat rolled out for business lobbyists.

In January 1962, President Kennedy's Economic Report of the President could still state, "There is a claim on our conscience from . . . the elderly, nonwhites, migratory workers, the physically or mentally handicapped people who are shortchanged even in time of prosperity." But in February 1973, President Nixon was exhibiting the true face of America. He was describing as a "dismal failure", and decrying the "paternalism, social exploitation and waste" of the antipoverty and other social programs of the 1960s.

The Office of Economic Opportunity was being dismantled. Previously appropriated funds for vital social purposes such as health programs for children, school lunches, milk programs, supplemental nutritional programs for pregnant and lactating mothers, and medical services were being impounded. The proposed 1973-1974 budget cut drastically or eliminated completely such social initiatives as Medicare, Medicaid, rent supplements, housing, Title One help for children from low income families, Head Start, Job Corps, community health centers, community action programs, legal aid for the indigent, and others.

The Bishops Council of the African Methodist Episcopal Church accused President Nixon of emasculating programs that had given "the dispossessed of our land a reason for hope," and denounced as "dehumanizing to take from the Americans those supportive programs . . . which have formed a small basis of hope in a raging sea of despair."

Representative Carl Albert of Oklahoma, Speaker of the House, characterized the President's budget as of "limited horizons . . . devoid of any great vision of America." Senator Harrison A. Williams, Jr., of New Jersey called it "contemptuous of the real needs of the American people."

Instead, we are given revenue sharing that then Governor Jimmy Carter of Georgia has denounced as a "cruel hoax" for the poor and relatively powerless.

In a letter to the President, Ralph Nader and representatives of nineteen public interest groups charged that the Administration "has wielded an ax" on social programs "without even applying a scalpel to corporate subsidy programs." An accompanying table demonstrated that the proposed outlays for 1974 for "human investment" (improving the skills of the poor through education, manpower, and other programs, as contrasted with "maintenance" spending that refers to food stamps, welfare and other forms of subsistence aid) had been cut ten percent or $500 million from 1973.

Citing the President's budget message, the public interest groups wrote, "If throwing dollars at problems can be wasteful in human resources problems, why aren't the billions handed over to the maritime, drug and defense industries included in your analysis." They sum up, "It seems an understatement to conclude that you are employing a double standard: frugality for needy people, extravagance for corporate interests."

When it came the turn of President Ford, more than half of his proposed cuts of $117 billion in the 1976 fiscal budget were in health or income programs for the poor, and in cost of living increases in pension programs.

Our government turns toward the "working stiffs," the underprivileged, a frozen face of insensitivity, stigmatizing them as drones and welfare cheats.

Toward the wealthy and powerful, however, our government turns a benign face of benevolence. If a system of public welfare is injurious to the poor, why should not a private welfare system of trust funds be equally injurious to its limited number of beneficiary heirs? Thorstein Veblem termed this "reputable futility," a synonym for socially approved idleness.

Our government is much more solicitous of the comfort of the rich than the shelter of the poor. It provides billions of dollars in discreet subsidy to the rich in suburbia, while the central cities are left to rot. For instance, in 1969, the $2.5 billion for urban freeways was a far greater subsidy to car owners who daily fled the central city than was the $175 million provided for mass transit to city dwellers. Home builders were helped, through FHA, etc., to build over ten million units for the rich and middle class, while less than one millions units of low cost housing were constructed for the poor.

Our government is against permissiveness, which is defined as blackmail by the welfare poor and weak accommodation of young dissenters. But it is permissive with the wasteful military establishment at the Pentagon, permissive with defense contractors, permissive with fund raisers who finance elections.

The "corporate welfare bum" is best observed in its most favorable habitat—the government contract. The government today is the economy's biggest buyer of goods and services. The instrument through which it operates is the contract, and since World War II the federal contract has rivaled subsidies, tariffs, taxes, regulation, and welfare programs as tools of government intervention in the economy. Thus we have the "Contract State."

We have the word of Gordon W. Rule, who was the director of the Procurement Control and Clearance Section of the Navy Materiel Command until he had the temerity to testify before the Congressional Subcommittee on Priorities and Economy in Government of the Joint Economic Committee, that the free enterprise system had broken down in the awarding of multibillion dollar defense contracts. He charged that major contracting had changed into a "quasi-welfare industry" and that a cozy incestuous relationship between Pentagon officers, contractors, and politicians was wasting millions of the taxpayers' dollars and making out of guns and bombs the biggest pork barrel in history.

Senator William Proxmire released the names of 131 contractors who were found in the fiscal year 1972 to have earned "exorbitant rates of return"—one as high as 1,900 percent return on net worth. Admiral Hyman G. Rickover, in testimony before a Senate-House Economic Committee in April 1975, charged that hundreds of millions of dollars in excessive profits had been made by defense contractors. He accused the Renegotiation Board of being "a sieve with large holes."

Competitive bidding on big government contacts has encouraged contractors to cut their prices sharply in an attempt to "buy in" on a contract with the expectation that somehow "Uncle Sugar" would ultimately bail them out.

Thus, between 1959 and 1973, the Department of Defense, under the emergency authorization of Public Law 85-804, awarded $85.9 million in outright grants to defense contractors, frequently without the ratification or even the knowledge of the Secretary of Defense.

Thus, the government guaranteed a $250 million bail-out loan to the Lockheed Aircraft Corporation after having arbitrarily increased earlier by one billion dollars the C5A and Cheyenne contracts. Thus, the Navy purchased all 17,414 shares of preferred stock in the Gap Instrument Corporation of Hauppauge, New York after the company ran into financial problems "attributed to inflation and too low an original bid by the company." Thus, the Navy also purchased $3.2 million of the convertible preferred stock of Applied Devices Corporation.

Senator William Proxmire accused the Navy of acting as the "private banker" of the Grumman Corporation in making fifty-four million dollars in private direct loans to the aircraft manufacturer. These loans were made despite the fact that the company, at the time, had refused to complete its contract to build forty-eight more F-14 fighter planes by going as far as mailing "stop work" orders to 130 subcontractors. This was despite a 1970 law that limited loans to any one company to $20 million unless Congress approved higher amounts.

In addition, the Defense Department has made substantial advance progress payments to Boeing, Litton, LTV, General Dynamics, and others, including four hundred million dollars to Lockheed. These and other contractors use thirteen billion dollars of plant equipment owned by the Department at nominal rentals.

Government contracts are perhaps the most obvious but certainly not the only form of "rip-off" of the public treasury.

For instance, farm subsidy programs, to remove acreages from cultivation so that housewives can pay more for their food, have cost taxpayers about fifty-eight billion dollars since they were begun in 1933. The 1972-1973 price tag was four billion dollars to keep twenty million farm acres idle, representing twenty-one percent of the nation's net farm income of nineteen billion dollars. The subsidy program was temporarily discontinued in 1973, but only after the price of food had soared to unprecedented levels because of the artificial scarcity and heavy exports.

Beginning in 1971, Congress decided to cut down farm subsidies for the rich and voted a limit of $55,000 per crop per farmer. This limitation turned out to be one huge farce. The big farmers simply subdivided their farms and created new entities. For instance, Senator James O. Eastland of Mississippi received $160,000 in 1970 for not growing cotton. In 1972, he met the $55,000 ceiling by creating eight subsidiaries and received $159,925 for not growing cotton.

Early in March 1971, Secretary of Agriculture Clifford M. Hardin announced that he would hold the line on milk prices and deny a price increase vigorously sought by farm dairy groups. On 23 March 1971, President Nixon met with dairy coop officials at the White House. Within twenty-four hours after this meeting, the Hardin order was reversed and the milk price rise, worth two hundred million to five hundred million dollars a year to the dairy farm industry, was granted. Coincidentally, hundreds of thousands of dollars in dairy farm contributions began to flow into the President's 1972 reelection campaign fund with at least $427,500 so tallied.

When beef prices fell, Congress, in July 1974, provided two billion dollars in loan guarantees to livestock producers. Cane and beet sugar growers were protected by quotas and received healthy subsidies, while sugar prices went through the roof.

In the year 1967, one-quarter of all commercial farmers received three-quarters of all subsidies—called equalization payments. The 264 largest received fifty-two million dollars, which sum was equal to that received by the 540,000 smallest farmers. In 1969, the wealthiest seven percent of farm owners received forty percent of all benefits while the poorest fifty percent received nine percent of benefits. Throughout, of course, the millions of landless farm workers received nothing.

A variety of Federal transportation subsidies, according to Senator William Proxmire of Wisconsin, chairman of the Subcommittee on Priorities and Economy in Government cost Americans about seven billion dollars annually. This does not take into account the hundreds of millions of dollars in welfare payments to Penn Central. It is the old story; "Socialize the losses and keep the profits private." Almost one billion dollars goes to the maritime industry. Air service to many small cities by "feeder airlines" is subsidized, as is the maintenance of airports, barge canals, port facilities, truck terminals, and highways. Amtrak is a direct handout to railroads, absorbing the cost of operating unprofitable passenger services.

Combined direct Federal subsidies to business add up to sixty-three billion dollars annually.

Traditionally, tariffs have been imposed to protect infant (and mature) industries. But the custom duty is only one of many devices utilized to shield domestic manufacturers from foreign competition—at the expense of the American consumer, of course. Among these are antidumping laws, unofficial (e.g. Japanese cotton, clothing and steel) and official quotas, (on sixty-seven industrial products), license fees, shipping restrictions, price supports, outright subsidies, and tax advantages (e.g. DISC and Western Hemisphere corporations).

For instance, on 1 May 1973, President Nixon terminated the controversial fourteen-year-old mandatory quotas on imports of oil. The Cabinet Task Force on Oil Import Control reported in 1969 that consumers were paying about five billion dollars more for oil products each year than they would have paid in the absence of such restrictions. It is doubtful whether the new license fees imposed in lieu of the quotas will lighten the burden of the consumer especially in view of the energy crisis.

To counter the abuses of private corporations vested with the public interest, such as railroads, airlines, banks, broadcasting, insurance, public utilities, and the like, regulatory legislation was enacted by the federal and state governments and regulatory agencies established to monitor corporate compliance. In no time at all, the regulatory agencies became the handmaidens of the companies to be regulated, so that if one looked first at the regulators and then at the regulatees, one was unable to distinguish one from the other. The result has been that the regulatory policies end up stifling competition and shielding utilities, banks, insurance companies, etc., from fair taxation and consumer demands.

Lewis A. Engman, chairman of the Federal Trade Commission, in an address to the Financial Analysts Federation in October 1974, declared, "Most regulated industries have become Federal protectorates, living in a world of cost-plus, safely protected from the ugly specters of competition, efficiency, and innovation. The result is that the consumer is paying plenty in the form of government sanctioned price fixing." Mr. Engman cited estimates that indicate that regulatory measures in transportation alone cost the consumer $16 billion a year. He concluded, "Our complex system of hidden regulatory subsidies make welfare fraud look like petty larceny."

Herbert S. Denenberg, the Insurance Commissioner of Pennsylvania, testified on 23 February 1973 before the Subcommittee on Antitrust and Monopoly of the Senate Judiciary Committee that life insurance was one "of the leading consumer frauds."

Every schoolboy is familiar with the Sherman and Clayton antitrust laws. But, in practice, these laws against monopolies, as we have seen earlier in this book, have not proven strong enough to prevent America from becoming a nation of giant enterprises with enormous power to fix prices, drive small competitors to the wall, create unemployment through restricted output, and stifle technological innovation.

The AFL-CIO is correct. There is a very real danger that America will eventually be turned into one enormous company-owned store. The solace of the all-powerful market has proven itself to be just another myth.

It is estimated that corporate parallel pricing, administered prices, target pricing, and lockstep pricing add up to eighty billion dollars in overcharges by shared monopolies that can set prices without regard to the laws of supply and demand. That estimate was made by Thomas E. Kaufer, head of the Justice Department Anti-Trust division. The companies in concentrated industries do not compete on prices, they simply match them.

It was Adam Smith who remarked in his *Wealth of Nations* in 1776 that, "People of the same trade rarely meet together, even for merriment and diversion, but the conversation ends in a conspiracy against the public or in some contrivance to raise the prices." Attorney General Edward Levi in June 1975 declared that the continual discovery of new price fixing cases tends to confirm a view that Adam Smith was probably right.

In January 1973, the Justice Department charged that top executives of the Ford Motor Company, General Motors, and Chrysler had held a series of secret meetings at which confidential cost information was exchanged.

Representing GM at these meetings was the chairman, Richard C. Gerstenberg. This is the same Mr. Gerstenberg who wrote in the *New York Times,*

> The future of our free enterprise economy is in his (the individual American's) hands. . . .By our actions we must demonstrate that free enterprise is the most effective instrument that man has ever devised for both economic and social progress.

This is the same Mr. Gerstenberg who hailed Phase 3 as "a return to the discipline of the competitive market." This is the same Mr. Gerstenberg who was the highest paid corporate executive in 1972, earning $874,963.

In October 1974 a Federal grand jury, sitting in Philadelphia, charged price-fixing on women's and men's apparel by prominent upper Fifth Avenue and Madison Avenue stores, including Bonwit's, B. Altman's, Bergdorf, and Saks Fifth Avenue, for as far back as 1935.

In August 1973, U.S. Steel, Bethlehem, Armco, and fourteen smaller companies were indicted on charges of price-fixing and market-sharing in the forty million dollar Texas market for steel reinforcing bars.

Have we forgotten the indictments handed down in February 1960 against twenty-nine corporations and forty-five executives in the electrical equipment manufacturing industry? Found guilty of price-fixing, bid-rigging and market-splitting, fines of $1,954,000 were levied, including $437,500 assessed against General Electric and $372,500 against Westinghouse. Fifteen manufacturers of plumbing fixtures were convicted on similar charges in 1969. Then, to add insult to injury, a private ruling by the Treasury (one out of thirty thousand each year) permitted the guilty companies to deduct the treble damages at a tax savings of $250 million.

Have we forgotten the 1968 suit by all fifty states and many cities against American Cyanamid, Bristol-Myers, Upjohn, Squibb, Beech-Nut and Pfizer for having conspired to fix the price of the antibiotic drug *tetracycline*? The drug companies settled for $174 million.

Have we forgotten that seven large manufacturers of gypsum wallboard were found guilty of fixing prices and bid-rigging between 1956 and 1968? And reindicted (and later convicted) in December 1973?

Have we forgotten the countless other cases of price-fixing and bid-rigging that are recorded in the dusty archives of our courts? Nothing escapes the attention of the price-fixers: dyes (yes, duPont), lettuce, paper labels (yes, International Paper), asphalt, even toilet seats, as well as fertilizers, bread and timber. You name it. What of the countless other conspiracies that never come to light?

Unfortunately, the abuses of corporate power surface too rarely for public scrutiny. Most of the time, the kind of power that monopoly interests hold is undramatic and technical. It is not proclaimed in public pronunciamentos. It is negotiated in dull court cases, insulated in the mazes of the Internal Revenue Code, buried in obscure pieces of legislation.

A researcher must come to the searing conclusion that corporate economic and environmental crimes dwarf other crimes in damage to the public health, safety, and property and in theft and confiscation of the people's treasure. As Woody Guthrie sang in "Pretty Boy Floyd", "As through this world I've rambled, I've seen lots of funny men. Some rob you with a six-gun and some with a fountain pen." Ralph Nader terms this white collar robbery with a fountain pen, "crime in the suites." Theodore Roosevelt used much stronger terminology. He called this group "malefactors of great wealth, the wealthy criminal class." Harry Truman, called them, "gluttons of privilege."

American corporate power has institutionalized corruption. Behind the manipulative deceptions that are the day-to-day practice of business lurk the capitalist desperados who loot the investing and consuming public in the great business scandals that headline our newspapers. The go-go years of 1969-1970 on Wall Street bilked thousands of small investors out of over $300 billion.

The ilk of Billy Sol Estes, Anthony DeAngelis, Albert Ponzi, Ivan Kruger, Lowell Birrell, C. Arnholt-Smith, Glenn Turner, Bernard Cornfeld, Robert Vesco, the Musica brothers, Samuel Insull, Jay Fiske, Equity Funding, Four Seasons Nursing Homes, Bunge Corp. grain scales, Minnie Pearl's chickens, Westec, and other so-called "ladies of the night" recur entirely too frequently to be accidental.

America is a society that has learned to live with dishonesty. Corruption is such a deep part of our daily life that it seems futile to try doing anything about it. Watergate, Vice President Agnew, the White House dirty tricks and horrors are but the other side of the coin. To quote Elliot L. Richardson, "A kind of sleaziness has infected the way things have been done, and this has touched agencies that have been concerned with law and law enforcement almost inevitably as part of the Government." To quote another public official who should know, Richard M. Nixon, "We find embezzlement, thievery, and criminal carelessness in American government."

There is always a Credit Mobilier, a Whisky Ring, a Teapot Dome, deep freezes, mink coats, vicuna coats, a Bobby Baker, and "the mess in Washington."

One can hardly pick up a newspaper any day without reading about some corporation, union, or public official that is being accused of graft or corruption. Even the arts are not spared—witness Clifford Irving.

Since the roles are interchangeable, one should not be surprised that the level of political morality had sunk to the low level of business morality. They are kindred spirits. When Mr. Agnew resigned, the Dow tumbled 13.62 points. Prime Minister Edward Heath speaks of "the unpleasant and unacceptable face of capitalism." Arnold Toynbee states that, "most of all in the United States, the standard of ethical conduct in business has sunk below the average standard in other kinds of social relations." William McChesney Martin, Jr. is shocked at the "lack of integrity in the market place," and David Babson complains that, "no greater period of skullduggery in American financial history exists than in 1967 to 1969."

All this covers an awful lot of time and territory. But it has always been thus. Adam Smith wrote that capitalists "generally have an interest to deceive and even to oppress the public." What does it matter if you cheat; everyone else is cheating too. Honoré de Balzac was not far off the mark when he observed that behind every fortune there is crime.

American capitalsim cannot function, cannot grow anymore without the use of illegal, illegitimate means. To a disturbing extent, business has become a vast network of rackets and gangs, powerful enough to bend the law or break it. The difference between the Mafia and legitimate business is becoming blurred: both exercise conspiratorial power.

Our institutions operate like a Robin Hood in reverse: to rob from the poor to give to the rich. Rape the poor is the slogan. Jacob Malik quotes an old Russian proverb to describe that what the United States is trying to do "is the same thing as a rich man; Taking the last shirt of the pauper."

Let's face it. Our economy, for its success, requires organized public bamboozlement. The selling of goods is a function of well-considered mendacity. Benjamin Franklin stated, "business is swindling." Professor William Z. Ripley of Harvard University once characterized corporate plundering to President Coolidge as "prestidigitation, double-shuffling, honey-fugling, hornswoggling and skullduggery." All too often, the business man emerges as the fakir, the juggler, the green goods man, the gold brick man. The modern princes of finance are in a class with the swindlers, dice-coggers and cutpurses of the Middle Ages.

Professor J.K. Galbraith argued in *The Affluent Society* (1958) that the paradox of public squalor amid private plenty derived from the capacity of major corporations, via the "dependency effect," to create demand for trivial merchandise by adroit advertising and promotion and the inability of public agencies to match these persuasive tactics. The result is wasteful misallocation of national resources.

It is worthwhile recording, with Charles A. Reich, who are the real socialists, collectivizers, and subversives in America; who are the enemies of the American way, the spoilers, the uprooters of tradition, the killers of the American dream. They do not have beards and bombs, accents and manifestos. They are, these enemies of the original American ideal, the pillars of our society, our great men, our captains of industry, our household heroes, our business men.

The costs of manufacture detailed on the profit and loss statements of industry do not list the true costs. Who pays for the environmental and human decay resulting from corporate operations? Who pays for the illness of the coal miner and the denuding of the hills of West Virginia? Who pays for the smog over Los Angeles and the strangling of Lake Erie? Who pays for the impoverishment that stems from the substitution of cigarettes, cosmetics, and souped-up automobiles huckstered by slick advertising agencies for the essentials of schools, housing, and health services? It would appear to the television viewer that the whole edifice of the corporate state is built on tranquilizers and sleeping pills.

Social accountability is a concept that is alien to corporate conduct. Business piracy, consumer deception, artificial shortages (meat and oil), unreliable products, false advertising and grotesque inequities have given a gangster cast to our economic world. While the very few wallow in spoils like rhinoceri in an African pool, the multitude struggles for sheer survival.

The laws themselves have lost any pretense of neutrality and have become a major weapon in the hands of the moneyed interests. Our legal system is not primarily concerned with justice, equity, or individual rights; it functions as an instrument of corporate domination. A sage once remarked that Law rules the poor and money rules the Law.

Specifically, as detailed in the next chapter, the tax laws are surely one of the most intricate and remarkable structures of inequity that the human mind has ever devised.

The old jingle comes to mind:

> The good old rule,
> The simple plan,
> That they should take who have the power
> And they should keep who can.

Yes, beyond any shadow of doubt, America *is* a welfare

state. But the free lunch counter is off limits for the hungry, the needy, the poor. The boodle is reserved for our plunder groups—the owners of America.

St. Augustine asked, "What are kingdoms without justice but bands of robbers?"

9

The Rape of the Taxpayer

By now, the gentle reader is justifiably complaining: this is supposed to be a book about taxes and here we've gone through half the book and the word "taxes" hasn't even been mentioned. The answer is that taxes are not imposed in a vacuum. Taxation, like welfare, is a political decision reflecting the distribution of power.

Before we can understand the rape of the taxpayer, we must understand the rape of the worker, the rape of the consumer, the rape of the young, the rape of the aged, the rape of the cities, the rape of the black, the rape of the citizen.

This chapter heading is taken from the book by Philip M. Stern published in 1973 by Random House. The subtitle of the book is "Why you pay more while the rich pay less."

Why should any citizen want to pay less than his fair share of the cost of running our country? Chiseled in stone above the main entrance of the Internal Revenue Service headquarters on Constitution Avenue in Washington is the quotation from Supreme Court Justice Oliver Wendell Holmes, "Taxes are what we pay for a civilized society." They are the insurance premiums for the protection afforded by the State. We cannot buy police protection, or fire protection, or jails, or an air force, or a navy, or parks, or welfare for the poor on our own. By paying taxes to a unit of government we provide for the purchase of these necessities.

Because these purchases are costly, taxes constitute a significant bite out of each individual's budget. According to the Tax Foundation, the average wage earner worked the first 121 calendar days of 1973—through 2 May—just to satisfy the tax collector. Put another way, two hours and thirty-nine minutes of the average American's eight-hour working day is used to earn money to pay taxes. By comparison, housing takes one hour's worth of work a day and food fifty-eight minutes. For the fiscal year ending 30 June 1973, federal, state, and local taxes took a total of $295 billion, or an average of $4,530, from every American household.

The combined budgets at the federal, state, and local levels account for about a third of the American gross national product. Of the overall total, state and local taxes amounted to $135 billion, or thirty percent. Thus, the lion share, or seventy percent, went to the Federal government to cover its budget of $349 billion. The largest proportion of the budget dollar—almost fifty cents—comes from individual income taxes—the center sheet anchor of the American financial system.

In the naive 1960s, the average citizen blissfully assumed that income taxes were progressive and were levied according to one's ability to pay. Thus, it was with a sense of shock that the public received the news on 17 January 1969 (three days before the Johnson administration left office) from Joseph Barr, who was Treasury Secretary for twenty-seven and one-half days at the end of that administration, that there were 155 tax returns in 1967 with adjusted gross incomes above $200,000 on which not one penny of federal income taxes had been paid. Included were twenty-one returns with income above one million dollars. Mr. Barr proceeded to warn of a "taxpayer revolt" unless the tax system was reformed.

It was all very embarrassing and out of the resulting public uproar there emerged eleven months later the 585 page

Tax Reform Act of 1969 and the new minimum tax. This imposes a special tax at a flat rate of ten percent on income that is given preferential treatment—either untaxed or lightly taxed—under the provisions of the tax law, provided the tax-free income exceeds $30,000 plus whatever tax the individual paid on his other income. Items of tax-preferred income that are subject to the minimum tax include accelerated depreciation deductions, income subject to depletion allowance, and the tax-free half of capital gain. The list does not include other tax-preferred items such as interest from state and local government bonds and income subject to the special deduction for oil and gas well drilling.

Despite the enactment of the 1969 law, in 1970, the first year of its application, a total of 3,314 persons with incomes of $30,000 or more still paid no income tax. Of these, 1,338 had incomes in excess of $50,000, 394 in excess of $100,000, 112 in excess of $200,000, 22 in excess of $500,000, and 3 in excess of $1,000,000. These are the mythical taxpayers who in fact receive hundreds of thousands of dollars in real income, but pay little or nothing in taxes.

However, the minimum tax did cost some 18,646 individuals a total of nearly $117 million in additional taxes in 1970 on preference income of $2,845,207,000—an average of only four percent.

In 1971, 276 individuals with adjusted gross incomes of $100,000 or more, 72 with $200,000 or more paid no Federal income tax. A total of 23,889 persons paid a minimum tax amounting to $163,887,000 on $3.9 billion of income that would not otherwise have been taxed at all. The average tax rate on the income subject to the minimum tax was thus 4.3 percent. Of those who did pay some minimum tax, 1,614 reported that they had no adjusted gross income.

The 1972 "zero taxpayers' list" boasted 402 individuals with incomes in excess of $100,000 who paid no tax, while in 1973, 870 individuals paid no income tax, although they had incomes over $200,000.

The reader should again be cautioned here concerning definitions. All official reports of income refer to adjusted gross income. This is the number you arrive at on your Form 1040 before you subtract your deductions. But percentages based on this number are misleading because items such as the untaxed half of net long-term capital gains, interest on tax-exempt municipal bonds, oil depletion, and accelerated depreciation are excluded before we reach the adjusted gross income line. It is thus possible to have very large amounts of tax-favored income, but little or no adjusted gross income. These taxpayers are not only escaping the tax collector, they are escaping the statisticians as well.

For example, the Internal Revenue figures for 1970 showed that there were 3,140 individuals who reported no adjusted gross income—in the aggregate, in fact, they showed a loss—but who had a total tax preference income of $197,245,000.

The number of persons who pay no income tax at all tells only a minute portion of the story. What of the substantially larger number of persons who pay a disproportionately low percentage of their income as taxes?

A glance at the income tax-rate schedule accompanying your tax form will disclose a noble progression of a graduated tax beginning with fourteen percent on taxable income over $500, for married couples filing jointly, and ranging up to seventy percent on taxable income over $200,000. This conforms with the principle enunciated by Adam Smith two centuries ago:

> The subjects of every state ought to contribute towards the support of the government as nearly as possible in proportion to their respective abilities, that is, in proportion to the revenue which they respectively enjoy under the protection of the state. The expense of government to the individual of a great nation is like the expense of management to the joint tenants of a great estate who are all obliged to contribute in proportion to their respective interests in the estate.

Nobly said, but what actually happens in real life? Considering taxes imposed by all levels of government, almost all American families pay about the same percentage of their income in taxes—twenty to twenty-five percent.

According to the Internal Revenue Service, the top one percent of taxpayers, with incomes of roughly $45,000 and up, have paid an average of only twenty-six percent of their total earnings, including capital gains, in recent years. The actual average effective rate of tax for individuals with incomes of over $100,000 is in the range of twenty-nine to thirty-three percent. The real tax rate of families with taxable income of $50,000 per year and over is the same as that of families with taxable income of $5,000.

Mr. Barr also told the same hearing of the Joint Economic Committee of the Congress that in 1968 taxpayers in the $7,000 to $20,000 taxable income bracket paid a higher percentage in taxes than the top one percent. For millionaires who paid income taxes in 1967, the effective rate was twenty-five percent.

Thus, Jean Paul Getty, one of the richest men in the world, who was worth between a billion and a billion and a half dollars, and who had a daily income of $300,000, is said to have paid only a few thousand dollars a year in income taxes. Mrs. Horace Dodge (of the Dodge auto fortune) received over five million dollars of income each year without even having to file an income tax return. Mr. Stern tells of a Mr. Nontaxpayer who earned five million dollars over seven years, yet paid only $4,509 in taxes. President Nixon disclosed that he paid only $792.81 in Federal income taxes for 1970, $878.03 for 1971, and $4,298 in 1972 despite an income average in excess of $280,000 per year. Averaged over the three years, the taxes were about what a $15,000 per year family would pay. Vice-President Nelson Rockefeller's total Federal tax, including income and gift taxes, amount to only 32.5 percent of his reported gross income over a ten-year period.

The rate in the tax schedules until 1975 for larger corporations with net income over $25,000 was 48 percent. However, such items as the special allowances for the oil industry, special capital gains tax treatment for the timber industry, special treatment for capital gains, and the off-again, on-again investment credit drop the actual average effective rate of tax for profitable corporations to around thirty-five percent. For the top one hundred corporations, according to Congressman Charles A. Vanik of Ohio, the rate is 27 percent. For some corporations, the rate is zero or close to it. In 1973 ten giant corporations with total profits of over $900 million paid no federal income tax at all.

In fact, especially since the Revenue Act of 1971, many corporations have achieved a state of near taxlessness.

In 1973, the six big oil companies reported net profits of $6.7 billion. Their average tax rate, however, was 9.5 percent. Texaco paid at the rate of 2.3 percent, Standard Oil of Ohio 3.5 percent, Mobil Oil 5 percent, Gulf 3.1 percent. The first award by the Tax Action Campaign of "Tax Avoider of the Week" went to the Shell Oil Company that in 1971 made $300 million in profit but paid only fifteen percent federal income tax. Although Atlantic-Richfield has earned $465 million in the four years through 1971, it has paid no federal income taxes.

Chase Manhattan paid an effective Federal income tax of 2.5 percent in 1973 while the comparable figure for American Express was 18.5 percent and for Gulf and Western 21 percent.

Among other "Tax Avoiders of the Week" cited by the Fred R. Harris Tax Action Campaign we find Alcoa, which paid no federal income tax for 1971; Georgia-Pacific, the timber-based conglomerate, which paid 11.3 percent, and Tenneco, another giant conglomerate, which paid 17 percent.

Given the statutory tax schedules, how do we account for the uneven incidence, the wide disparities in the tax rate imposed on different corporations and individuals? The answer, of course, is the loopholes bored into the tax law.

Thus, Mr. Stern cautions that those who blame high tax rates exclusively on excessive government spending are, to a considerable extent, hissing the wrong villain. They should reserve at least some of their indignation for the prodigiously costly tax loopholes and preferences.

Dr. Joseph A. Pechman, director of economic studies at Brookings Institution, in an interview published in the *New York Times* of 17 January 1972, groped for a suitable analogy for the inequities of the tax system. He first suggested a sieve but then dismissed that term because a sieve has too much substance and the holes are too small. He finally settled on a fish net with holes big enough to let any determined fish slip through. In actual practice, there is more loophole than law, permitting many big taxpayers to escape scot-free while grinding ever more money out of the small fry. In his book *The Public Interest,* Dr. Pechman called the tax system a "disgrace."

Other authorities have used even stronger language. Senator Frank Lausche called the tax system a "fraud," Wilbur Mills, long term chairman of the House Ways and Means Committee, characterized it as a "house of horrors," "a gyp," "riddled with preferential benefits." George Meany, president of the American Federation of Labor and Congress of Industrial Organizations, stated, "What we've got in this country is a tax swindle."

Our Byzantine, bizarre tax structure is a public-relations gimmick. Our tax rates bark far more than they bite. Tough, artificially high tax rates are voted in bold print with great fanfare and then made meaningless by the fine print. Enormous surtaxes are voted in exchange for promises that they will not be made effective. Since a bold, frontal assault on the tax law, openly proclaiming tax preferences so as to lessen the tax burden of a select and favored group of taxpayers would be too offensive to American economic folklore, the real purpose is beclouded by a camouflaged flank attack on the steeply graduated rate schedules.

The whole procedure smacks of moral and political dishonesty. The politicians publicly point with pride to the high rates, while quietly reminding their wealthy campaign contributors of the loopholes.

The resulting 1,856 pages of the Internal Revenue Code, with its over 4,000 pages in supporting regulations, are, according to tax authority Louis Eisenstein, "a remarkable essay in sustained obscurity" with "all the earmarks of a conspiracy in restraint of understanding"—designedly so. Even as brilliant a jurist as Learned Hand remarked that the words of the tax law "merely dance before my eyes in a meaningless procession, couched in abstract terms that offer no handle to seize hold of." Senator Sam Ervin commented that any person who could interpret the tax laws could "unscrew the unscrutable."

The law is so complicated that an estimated 40 million taxpayers have to turn to accountants and lawyers for help in preparing their returns at an annual cost of $600 million. A report filed by the House Government Operations Committee (H Rept. 93-600) estimated 250,000 such preparers in 1973.

Martin A. Larson, in his book *The Great Tax Fraud,* characterized the Internal Revenue Code as follows:

> Based presumably on the concepts of equality and justice, it is the most effective diabolical instrument ever devised for fleecing the honest and the industrious and for enriching the crafty and the parasitical.

According to Representative Henry S. Reuss, Democrat of Wisconsin, "The minimum tax is itself filled with loopholes."

What are these nefarious loopholes?

In May 1972 Representative Wilbur Mills introduced the Tax Policy Review Act of 1972, a bill promptly forgotten and never heard of again. That legislation would have gradually repealed, over a three-year period beginning in 1974, 54 special provisions of the tax law that are commonly termed loopholes. The idea was to set terminal dates for the various tax preferences thus forcing the Congress to specifically reenact each one; modify it or let it die.

The Budget Reform Act of 1974 required the President to itemize these so-called tax expenditures. Such a table appears as "Special Analysis F" beginning on page 101 of *Special Analyses: Budget of the United States Government: Fiscal Year 1976*. The tax expenditures—or loopholes, if you will—total $91 billion, equivalent to one-fourth of what President Ford estimated the Government would spend in all.

It is clear that tax expenditures overwhelmingly favor the upper bracket taxpayer. A Treasury Department study showed that the 14.6 percent of taxpayers who made more than $20,000 in 1974 received 53 percent of the benefits from tax loopholes. On the average, based on 1972 estimates, a taxpayer at the $3,000 to $5,000 level received $10 in tax expenditure assistance; in the $25,000 to $50,000 bracket, $1,358; in the $100,000 to $500,000 slot, $29,264; and in the $1,000,000 bracket, $725,000.

Listed below are some of the major tax expenditures and the cost of each to the Treasury. The reader should consider each one of these preferences as if it were a direct government expenditure. A dollar foregone through a special tax provision is no different than a dollar spent through a budget outlay. President Nixon stated in his 1972 budget message,

> Every dollar in taxes that some individual or industry is excused from paying is just as much of a drain on the Treasury, and contributes just as much to Federal deficits, as a dollar appropriated by the Congress and spent directly from the Treasury.

For instance, take capital gains: this category, like Abou ben Adhem, leads all the rest. The profit on the sale of capital assets—stocks, real estate, bonds, other investment assets—held for over six months (nine months in 1977) is taxed at only one-half the regular rate of taxation. But since only one taxpayer in 12 is able to report such gains, and since three-quarters of the gains are enjoyed by the wealthiest 9 percent of taxpayers, we have here the most gaping escape hatch for the very rich.

A Brookings Institution study authored by Mr. Pechman and Benjamin Okner calculated what they called the "tax welfare" payments—the average per family tax savings—granted capital gains recipients by income level:

YEARLY INCOME	YEARLY TAX WELFARE PER FAMILY FROM CAPITAL GAINS
Over $1,000,000	$641,000
$500,000 to $1,000,000	165,000
$100,000 to $500,000	23,000
$20,000 to $25,000	120
$15,000 to $20,000	55
$5,000 to $10,000	8
$3,000 to $5,000	1

It should be kept in mind that incomes over $100,000 are earned by only 78,000 families comprising two-tenths of one percent of all taxpayers, while incomes over $1,000,000 are earned by only 3,000 families.

The higher a family's total income, the greater the proportion of that income that is made up of capital gains. For instance:

INCOME GROUP	PERCENT OF PEOPLE IN THIS INCOME GROUP WITH CAPITAL GAINS	PERCENT OF INCOME REPRESENTED BY CAPITAL GAINS
Under $5,000	4.5%	1.9%
$10,000-$25,000	14.0	2.4
$50,000-$100,000	55.3	15.6
$1,000,000 and over	90.9	82.1

According to the Tax Reform Research Group, for the 12.6 million taxpayers in the $7,000 to $10,000 income bracket an average savings of only $15.07 a year was realized as a result of the special tax treatment of capital gains. For those in the $10,000 to $15,000 bracket, the average savings was $23.27; those in the $15,000 to $20,000 group averaged

$52.67; and those in the $20,000 to $50,000 bracket $284.59. But for the 91,286 persons in the over $100,000 category in 1971, this savings averaged $39,211.

These handouts to the wealthy as a result of the special capital gain treatment reach the astounding total of $13.7 billion annually.

Further, gains in the value of property a person holds until death was not taxed at all until 1977. Some $10 billion escaped taxation entirely in this manner every year. The capital gains preference also plays a key role in the tax shelters we will discuss later.

Dramatically top-heavy tax largesse flows to the super-rich via the fiction in the tax law that the over $6 billion of interest on state and municipal bonds is totally nonexistent. Not only is such interest income untaxed, it does not even have to be reported on tax returns. As was noted above, ownership of these bonds is reserved almost exclusively to the wealthy and to banks. This special tax treatment yields annual tax savings averaging only 71 cents for those in the $10,000 to $15,000 bracket and a handsome financial blessing of $36,000 a year for families with incomes of over $1 million. In 1970 this tax feature saved the Bank of America an estimated $58 million. The total price tag to the Treasury adds up to $4 billion.

Students of the subject contend that the tax exemption is a grossly inefficient means of subsidizing state and local borrowing costs since the states and cities save less than $3 billion in reduced interest rates. Both tax justice and governmental economy would be better served by replacing the tax exemption with a direct subsidy program.

In addition to this municipal bond interest, which is legally nonreportable, it is estimated that another $6 billion in interest and dividend income is similarly not being shown on income tax returns, illegally this time, at a taxpayer cost of $1 billion.

We have already mentioned the phantom oil depletion allowance. Schedule F lists $3 billion for this item. Since then, the Congress, in 1975, voted to repeal this allowable deduction for the big oil companies and reduce it for the smaller ones.

The generosity of our Government to business does not stop there. Through the tax structure, the United States taxpayer subsidizes foreign subsidiary operations of American corporations. These corporations pay no income taxes here on profits of foreign subsidiaries until such profits are brought back home—which may be never. Further, foreign tax credits until 1975 allow taxes paid to foreign governments to be deducted dollar for dollar from the corporation's United States taxes—something that cannot even be done with state and local taxes on income that are simply additional expenses. Because of such deferrals and credits, United States corporations operating abroad paid only $900 million in 1970 on $17.5 billion in profits, an effective rate of only five percent. The cost of these tax subsidies favoring overseas operations is put at $3 billion. Thus, the Treasury reported that the oil companies, in 1971, had cut their taxes from $3.2 billion to $799 million because of the tax-credit system. And the irony of it is that these credits were supposed to insure an uninterrupted supply of oil from Saudi Arabia. As a result, this rule was also changed in 1975.

The Revenue Act of 1971 included three bonanzas for business: A speed-up method of treating depreciation of equipment, an investment credit to offset part of the cost of equipment purchases, and a deferral of taxation on one-half of the income of export corporations through so-called Domestic International Sales Corporations (DISC). These business tax-giveaways cost United States taxpayers $7.2 billion a year. Representative Vanik declared that, with the passage of this Act, the Administration and Congress were moving toward "dismemberment of the corporate tax system."

Top corporate executives, doctors, lawyers, and other professionals with earned taxable incomes of $40,000, if single, and $55,000, if married, are taxed at a maximum rate of fifty percent. This preference for those whose income is derived from high salaries and fees costs $200 million. The theory is that if taxes on the wealthy are cut, they will not try quite so hard to find loopholes.

We mentioned above the disproportionate concentration of stock holdings among the super-rich. Thus, it was to be expected that the tax-free status of the first $100 of dividends received each year by an individual would yield a tax savings of only $3.90 to the average person in the $10,000 to $15,000 class, and of $115.53 to the average taxpayer in the over $100,000 bracket. This preference saves wealthy taxpayers $320 million a year.

Even tax favors granted to the lowly, as well as to the mighty, result in inequity. While the supposed purpose of the $750 personal exemption available to each taxpayer and his dependents is to spare poor families from being taxed on what is necessary to meet minimum living costs, this feature benefits the rich more than the poor. A top-bracket Rockefeller or Mellon gets $525 of benefit for each personal exemption—five times the $105 of benefit accruing to the lowest bracket slum dweller. This exemption confers some $4 billion in tax handouts to families making over $15,000 a year.

The same perversity applies to the additional $750 exemption that Congress has voted the aged and the blind.

Supposedly as an incentive to marriage and the family, at that happy moment when a couple is pronounced man and wife, our Government bestows upon them as a wedding present the privilege of filing a joint return. This means that the combined income is split down the middle and the tax is calculated at the resulting lower average bracket. If the purpose of this provision is to encourage marriage, it moves its wonders to perform in strange ways. For it shows a total indifference to the many poor who derive no financial benefit from this tax giveaway. Instead, it offers increasingly generous benefits the higher a couple's income goes, in brackets where it matters little whether two can indeed live as cheaply as one.

Two-thirds of this marital tax welfare goes to taxpayers making more than $20,000 a year and less than three percent goes to the hardest pressed married couples—the forty-six percent of families earning less than $10,000 a year. These are the average per family matrimonial tax savings:

YEARLY INCOME	YEARLY TAX WELFARE TO MARRIED COUPLES
Under $3,000	None
$3,000-$5,000	.72 cents
$5,000-$10,000	$ 24.00
$25,000-$50,000	1,479.00
$100,000-$500,000	8,212.00
Over $1,000,000	11,062.00

The enormous sum of $21.5 billion would be raised by abolishing the privilege of filing joint returns.

The upside-down results of a number of tax breaks designed to encourage social goals is illustrated by the tax-law provision permitting a deduction for mortgage interest. This deduction is granted to stimulate home ownership. Yet the Brookings Institution concludes that the various tax preferences enjoyed by homeowners over home-renters come to just 66 cents a year for the least pecunious taxpayers who need housing the most and 10,000 times as much—over $6,000 a year for the wealthiest and best-housed families. The mansion dweller derives much more benefit from this preference than the Levittowner.

The price tag attached to this inverted subsidy program, $6.5 billion a year, is more than twice HUD's total budget and more than fifty times HUD's direct outlays for housing assistance.

Similarly, with regard to property taxes, the per taxpayer savings for those in the $10,000 to $15,000 bracket averaged $45.52 a year, whereas in the over $100,000 bracket the savings averaged $1,758.66. The overall cost of the deductibility of state and local taxes is $5.6 billion.

These inequities extend to any number of other tax deductions. A parishioner in the top bracket who drops one dollar in the church collection basket is only dropping 30 cents; his poor neighbor is actually dropping 86 cents. The Treasury contributes $3.8 billion each year as its share of taxpayer donations, 66.7 percent of which went to the 14.6 percent of taxpayers earning over $20,000 per annum.

As we have seen, the minimum-tax administers a small love pat to wealthy tax avoiders. Having paid this small admission fee for the privilege, the high-salaried executive and the highly paid professional stand at the threshold of the wide open spaces entitled tax shelters.

In fact, ingenious tax lawyers have developed a whole new line of business whose sole product is the packaging and merchandising of tax shelters—ranging from oil drilling and apartment houses, to avocado or kiwi nut groves, motion pictures, cattle ranches, and hobby farms, none of which the investor ever sees. Business journals advertise so-called tax shelter conferences.

What these tax shelters have in common is that they provide a means of taking large deductions each year (often in excess of the money outlay) against the income that the investor earns from other sources and that would otherwise be taxed at high, progressive, ordinary income rates. The deductions may be for interest, the cost of feed, farm and timber outlays, local taxes, depreciation, drilling, or other items. But when the time comes to sell the investment, any increase in its value is taxed at the capital-gains rate.

Wilbur Mills has said that these Wall Street cowhands, armchair oil drillers, city farmers, and wealthy investors who buy tax deductions are making a "travesty" of the tax laws. This flourishing business of peddling expertise in tax avoidance mocks any argument that the tax code works fairly and needs no overhaul. This travesty costs us—you and I—one billion dollars a year.

When all else fails, we can trust those who are acquisitive, successful, and ruthless enough to create huge incomes or to amass vast fortunes to be capable of protecting both by enlisting or buying the services of Congressmen to plant tailor-made new escape hatches in the revenue code. This legerdemain is accomplished through the medium of "members' bills." These are tax bills sponsored by a member of the House Ways and Means Committee intended to effect just one industry or one company or one individual. Generally, as a matter of Congressional courtesy, such legislation has been enacted with little or no debate.

Such special provisions in tax bills never name the taxpayer they aim to benefit, but the requirements are so narrow and precise that only the intended beneficiary fits the escape hatch. Thus, Section 49(b) (10) on page 420 of the Tax Reform Act of 1969 had been specifically custom-tailored and specially inserted into the bill on behalf of a single company; Uniroyal, Inc., the nation's sixty-eight largest corporation. The 310-page committee report contained no hint of this special provision that spelled a tax savings of about 3 million dollars to the corporation.

A special provision, Section 1240, enacted in 1951, saved Louis B. Mayer 2 million dollars in taxes, and one enacted in 1956 saved 4 million dollars for the estate of Mary Hill Swope, the widow of Gerard Swope, former president of General Electric. Among numerous other such pieces of legislation, we have a half billion-dollar tax gift to IBM, and the bail-out of duPont on their disposition of General Motors stock. Other beneficiaries of "members' bills" have been Litton Industries, Lockheed, McDonnell-Douglas, Mobil Oil, Gwendolyn Capritz, Ellsworth C. Alvord, Leo Sanders, the Cannon Foundation, the Twin Cities Rapid Transit Company, and the estate of Charles E. Merrill of Merrill, Lynch—to name only a few.

We have not discussed but should note, such tax-related goodies that fall to the wealthy as deferred compensation, stock options, medical reimbursement, life insurance, pension and profit-sharing, company planes, and vacation chalets, expense accounts, and other schemes that are the product of fertile tax minds.

Existing federal estate and gift tax laws provide innumerable exemptions and a host of opportunities to avoid, minimize, or postpone tax payments through devices such as family foundations, generation skipping trusts, and marital deductions. Filed estates of over 1 million dollars average only seventeen percent in taxes. Even the estates of the big rich approximate only twenty-seven percent in death taxes. These rates, of course, are far below the published estate-tax schedules. It is estimated that an overhaul of estate and gift taxes would yield 3 billion dollars annually to the Treasury.

Perhaps it is just as well that Mr. Mills' tax-reform proposals never saw the light of day. In the past, as Mr. Stern notes, every time the tax tent is cracked another inch, a dozen more camels' noses instantly present themselves crying, "Me, too." Louis Eisenstein remarked that tax equity is the privilege of paying as little as the next fellow. Loopholes beget loopholes like a chain reaction of tax favors.

Of necessity, this review of loopholes had to be quite cursory. We have not discussed many other preferences such as the exemption of $15,000 for those living abroad, retirement income credit, family income splitting, moving expenses, nontaxability of sale of a residence, etc., etc. But there are many books on the library shelves dealing with loopholes that are readily available to the reader. An excellent book is *Halfway To Tax Reform* by Joseph A. Ruskay and Richard A. Osserman, published in 1970 by the Indiana University Press, with a Foreword by Congressman Henry S. Reuss.

10

To Him Who Has

The functioning of the tax law upholds the wisdom of the Biblical aphorism that "from him who has not shall be taken away and to him who has shall be given."

When the first full-fledged income tax proposal was introduced on the floor of the United States Senate in 1894, Senator John Sherman called it an "attempt to array the poor against the rich that will lead to socialism, communism, and devilism." When the Sixteenth Amendment was adopted a New York Times editorial, on 2 April 1913, charged that the new tax "transferred the burdens of the many to the shoulders of the few."

The fact is that the operation of the income tax act has proven the exact opposite. The rich are not being soaked. Instead, they are soaking up wealth very rapidly in ever-increasing amounts. Beyond the shadow of a doubt, the tax code helps the rich grow richer. It gives crumbs to the poor and gravy to the rich. It is the most blatant exercise of a soak-the-poor conspiracy.

Here is the perfect example of power begetting money. Here is the perfect example of the workings of the welfare state.

The effect of the tax expenditures, loopholes, preferences, and favors embedded in the nation's tax laws is identical to the effect of handing direct welfare checks to the wealthy families and corporations. One man's loopholes is another man's cross. The wealthy end up wealthier, the Treasury ends up poorer, and the rest of the taxpayers have to make up the difference. These handouts can rightfully be called "tax welfare payments."

In January 1972, experts Pechman and Okner made a computer analysis for the Brookings Institution of information from actual tax returns furnished to them on computer tape, without taxpayer names, by the Internal Revenue Service. Using this data, they calculated the average yearly tax-welfare payment per family by income grouping:

YEARLY INCOME	TAX WELFARE
Over $1,000,000	$720,000
$500,000-$1,000,000	$202,000
$100,000-$500,000	$ 41,000
$50,000-$100,000	$ 12,000
$25,000-$50,000	$ 4,000
$15,000-$25,000	$ 1,200
$10,000-$15,000	$ 650
$5,000-$10,000	$ 340
$3,000-$5,000	$ 48
Under $3,000	$ 16

As we can see, they concluded that just 92 million dollars, or sixteen dollars a year, per family, goes to the six million poorest families in the nation, while twenty-four times that amount or $2.2 billion, goes to the three thousand families with incomes in excess of one million dollars annually. For this privileged class, the average yearly tax handout is an unbelievable $720,000 per family or almost $14,000 a week, $2,000 a day.

For the richest three families in every one-thousand or 200,000 out of the 70.4 million families in the country, the tax welfare payments amount to $11.4 billion as follows:

INCOME GROUP	PERCENTAGE OF POPULATION	PERCENTAGE OF TAX WELFARE PAYMENTS
Under $10,000	45.7%	10.0%
Under $15,000	70.6%	24.7%
Over $100,000	0.3%	14.7%

Considered another way, \$11.4 billion is about twice what the Federal government spends on food stamps, thirty-four times the outlay on cancer research, seven times that on all medical research, ten times the cost of school lunches, seven times the budget of the Federal Environmental Protection Agency.

What happened?

Like so many other facets of American society, income taxes started out from a position of equality. The Sixteenth Amendment to the Constitution empowered Congress to tax "incomes, from whatever source derived." The naive student would assume that a dollar is a dollar is a dollar, and that the dollar derived from wages would be as efficacious in buying groceries and shoes and a college education as a dollar derived in an oil venture or a stock-market bonanza. Does not the number of dollars you receive in income determine your ability to pay?

As Will Rogers noted a long time ago, "it ain't necessarily so that them what's got pays the taxes." To paraphrase George Orwell, all income dollars are equal but some have become more equal than others. In the past sixty-odd years, the Internal Revenue Code has developed a bias toward capital rather than to human toil. George McGovern was so right when he declared that money made by money was not taxed at the same rate as money made by man. Ours is a welfare state structured in favor of those who make money by investing money. Its goal is to concentrate wealth in the hands of those who do not produce, while taking it from the hands of those who do.

Our tax structure is rigged against income from work and against wage and salary earners. It is rigged in favor of unearned income and the loophole set. The vast majority of taxpayers, whose taxes are withheld from their paychecks and whisked away before they even see the money, are largely helpless. They never even get a chance to pursue the loopholes.

Here is the best proof of the fact that taxation is a political process. Our tax system reflects a continuing struggle among contending interests for the privilege of paying the least in taxes. Class politics is the essence of taxation and, to date, in the United States, the moneyed classes have prevailed. The result, as we have seen, is pillage of the unpropertied by the governing propertied class. The poor, for all practical purposes, are subsidizing the rich. The poor are the patsies. Alan A. Tait terms the American tax system a fraud manipulated by the legal and political hired guns of the vested interests in order to reinforce the power of wealth in this country.

J.P. Morgan said,

> Anybody has a right to evade taxes if he can get away with it. No citizen has a moral obligation to assist in maintaining the government. If Congress insists on making stupid mistakes and passing foolish tax laws, millionaires should not be condemned if they take advantage of them.

There is no record of anyone inquiring at whose behest the "stupid mistakes" were made and the "foolish tax laws" passed.

Mr. Morgan's concept has been frozen into the law. Judge Learned Hand declared in Commissioner v. Newman (1947),

> There is nothing sinister in so arranging one's affairs as to keep taxes as low as possible. Everybody does so, rich or poor; and all do right. Nobody owes any public duty to pay more than the law demands: taxes are enforced exactions, not voluntary contributions. To demand more in the name of morals is mere cant.

Congressman John Davis of Kansas once said, "The millionaire pays the least tax and is the most expensive man in the country."

The 1969 Economic Report of the President presented data showing that the combined federal, state, and local tax systems converge in such a manner as to redistribute income away from the poor. At the same time, those of modest and middle incomes are bearing a disproportionately high share of the tax burden, while those with wealth and ability to pay escape their fair share. The ingenuity of our tax lawyers has been so exercised that the wages of labor are drained in such small amounts and in such insidious modes that the working man does not even realize that he is paying taxes, much less take the trouble to remonstrate effectively.

The one tax that was supposed to fall more heavily upon the rich is the graduated income tax. Economists call it a "progressive" tax in contrast to sales, payroll, and property taxes that bear more heavily on the poor and, hence, are "regressive." Yet, the graduated income tax has been reduced no less than six times since the Korean war to the tune of forty-two billion dollars a year. For example, Leon Keyserling analyzed the percentage gains to various income groups as a result of the 1964 personal income tax cut. The person earning $3,000 per year benefited 2 percent; $5,000, 1.6 percent; $7,500, 2.1 percent; $10,000, 2.3 percent; $25,000, 3.8 percent; $50,000, 6.2 percent; $100,000, 8.3 percent; $200,000, 16 percent.

On the contrary, as a welcome change, the 1974 and 1975 acts reduced taxes 238 percent for the poorest, 103 and 51 percent for the next poorest classes, 15 to 28 percent for the middle class and below 6 percent for the wealthy.

While income taxes were being reduced, sales, payroll, and similar overtly regressive taxes have been increased repeatedly. In the past twenty years, local taxes have grown from seven percent to twelve percent of the gross national product. The following table taken from the 1969 Economic Report of the President shows dramatically the percentage of income represented by state and local taxes for various income classes in 1965:

FAMILY INCOME	PERCENTAGE OF INCOME PAID IN STATE AND LOCAL TAXES
Under $2,000	25%
$2,000-$6,000	10.5%
$6,000-$10,000	9%
Over $15,000	7%

Herman P. Miller of the Census Bureau reports that the overall effective tax rate on a poor family ($2,000 a year) and a rich family ($50,000 a year) is currently about the same—approximately one-third—when the burden of sales, payroll, and similar taxes is considered. These conclusions were supported by the Thurow-Lucas study, which we will discuss later, where it was found that progressive taxes are cancelled by regressive taxes, leaving a proportionate tax system.

The one tax that is rising faster than any other Federal tax is the Social Security tax, one of the most regressive taxes that Americans pay. The maximum tax here has risen from $60 in 1949 to $895.05 in 1976. Millions of workers who pay no Federal income tax, because of low income allowances and the like, pay 5.85 percent of their wages in Social Security taxes.

In 1963, payroll taxes collected amounted to forty-two percent of personal income taxes. By 1973, this percentage had climbed to sixty-eight percent. Dr. Pechman comments,

> Making the poor subject to payroll tax is a crime; the thing to do with payroll taxes is exempt the poor and raise the amount we pay. Finally, after all these years, people are picking up the idea that Social Security is a poor tax. The poor pay the same rate as you and I, but they pay it on all their earnings and we pay it on only a portion of our earnings—and that's the definition of a regressive tax.

Dr. Pechman believes that even the employer's portion of the Social Security tax falls eventually on the workers either as a substitute for larger wage increases or through inflated prices.

The Brookings Institution's 1973 budget study had suggested personal exemptions in the Social Security tax to ease the burden on the working poor and the lower middle class.

From a reading of the public press, one is led to believe that the United States is a welfare state because it lavishes all sorts of benefits upon the lazy shiftless poor who do not want to work. Actually, however, this make-believe welfare state costs the members of the ruling upper class virtually nothing. It is the lower classes who pay for Social Security, Medicare, and home relief through their payroll and sales taxes.

It is not necessary to belabor the point. The record speaks for itself. Yet apologists for the Administration, including former Secretary of the Treasury Connally, former presidential senior staff assistant Ehrlichman, former assistant Secretary of the Treasury for Tax Policy Cohen, and former assistant Secretary of the Treasury Hickman, took to the airways, in a display of sheer demagoguery, to argue that the only tax reforms that would raise large amounts of money would hurt the average taxpayer if "you don't let the average house holder deduct the interest on his mortgage anymore, and you don't let him deduct charitable contributions to his church or to the Boy Scouts." Mr. Connally had the effrontery to deny that any loopholes even exist, calling the special privileges "essential social instruments," while Mr. Cohen warned that tax reform would imperil the economy, and Mr. Connally that the Dow-Jones Industrial Index would fall to five hundred.

Robert Brandon, of the Tax Reform Research Group, charged that Nixon administration officials and Wilbur Mills had "tried to cover up the unfairness of the nation's tax laws." He said, "Those responsible for our unfair tax system are perpetrating a cruel hoax on the American people and assertions that average taxpayers are the major beneficiaries of our present tax loopholes are completely false."

Tax expert Stanley S. Surrey, a Harvard law professor who served as assistant treasury secretary in the Johnson administration, told the House Ways and Means Committee in February 1973 that the public outcry would be deafening if the average man knew how and by how much the rich and privileged are escaping taxes. He testified,

> These situations are an offense to our sense of fairness and decency. This is why tax reform is really a moral issue. It is not just a technical exercise to be engaged in by skilled experts. It is an effort to restore fundamental morality to a tax system by

ending both its unfairness and the cynical, immoral way the tax game is played today by those with money and knowledgeable advisers.

Public advocates like Fred Harris, Ralph Nader, Martin A. Larson, John Gardner, Thomas F. Field, Philip Stern, Robert Brandon, and others have undertaken the task of informing the taxpayers as to how present tax laws cheat and punish them. It is hoped that the public will respond with a great scream of fury once they realize the situation. It was Thomas Jefferson who said,

> Whenever the people are well informed, they can be trusted with their own government; whenever things get so far wrong as to attract their notice, they may be relied upon to set them to rights.

Otherwise, we shall have to write-off income taxes as another noble experiment that went awry. Randolph Paul called the income tax "a wasting asset of the nation." Diogenes, the pseudonym of an Internal Revenue agent turned author, concluded that degeneration seems to be built into the very meat and bones of income taxation just as aging and bodily decay and eventual death are built into the future of every human at birth.

Once, graduated income taxes were heralded as the white dove of economic democracy that would take from the rich their filthy, ill-gotten lucre, and redistribute it so that the poor and the disadvantaged might enjoy the more abundant life. The income tax grew out of a long period of progressive agitation and public disapproval of the vast fortunes of the new industrial rich in the face of the poverty and deprivation of the working class. Its avowed aim was redistribution.

Income taxes did not burst forth full blown on 13 February 1913 when Wyoming became the thirty-sixth state to ratify the Sixteenth Amendment to the Constitution. This form of tax has a long and venerable history.

Britain had adopted its first income tax on 9 January 1799 when William Pitt was prime minister. France had imposed such a tax two years earlier. The Swiss law dates back to 1840, Austria to 1849, Italy to 1864, Australia to 1884, New Zealand to 1891, Japan to 1887, Prussia to 1891 and the Netherlands to 1893.

Among the colonies, Massachusetts had imposed an income tax as early as 1646, and Rhode Island as early as 1672. After statehood, North Carolina adopted such an impost in 1849, followed by Alabama and Virginia. In 1815, Alexander J. Dallas, the Secretary of the Treasury, made the first call for a Federal income tax, claiming, "there are many wealthy men who do not contribute in due proportion to the public exigencies."

The first United States income tax was included in the second war internal revenue measure signed by President Lincoln on 1 July 1862. A tax of three percent on incomes from $600 to $10,000 from whatever source derived and of 5 percent on incomes in excess of $10,000 was imposed. This Civil War income tax was repealed on 3 March 1871 on the last day of that year's Congressional session. The constitutionality of that levy was upheld by the United States Supreme Court in Springer v. United States (1880).

The income tax next appeared as an amendment to the Wilson Tariff bill that became law on 28 August 1894 without the signature of President Cleveland. This act was declared unconstitutional in Pollock v. Farmers Loan and Trust Co. (1895), Justice Field terming the tax "class legislation." This decision necessitated the adoption of the Sixteenth Amendment. That amendment was implemented by the Internal Revenue Act of 3 October 1913.

The 1913 act, authored by Representative Cordell Hull, was a graduated tax with the normal tax starting at one percent in the $3,000 to $20,000 bracket. There was also a surtax that went up to six percent on taxable incomes over $500,000. A one percent tax was levied against corporate net income.

We have lived with income taxes ever since.

Similarly, inheritance taxes have been part of the American scene for a long time. The first death taxes were stamp taxes on petitions for probate of wills and the resulting transfer of legacies, and these go back to 1797. The second Civil War internal revenue measure also carried an inheritance tax of three-quarters of one percent to five percent on devised personalty in excess of $1,000, depending upon the degree of consanguinity of the beneficiaries. This tax was extended to real property in 1864. The entire tax was repealed in 1870.

The Revenue Act of 1898, enacted to finance the Spanish American War, contained an estate tax that was levied on the entire estate, not only on legacies, and carried a progressive rate structure. This legislation, which was repealed in 1902, was upheld in Knowlton v. Moore (1900). The current inheritance tax dates from 1916; William Pitt's government caused the enactment of the first British tax on legacies in 1805.

Here again, our review of tax legislative history, of necessity, had to be most cursory. For the interested reader, there are many books that will provide an excellent background. One such is *Taxation in the United States*, written by Randolph E. Paul and published in 1954 by Little Brown.

Read the record. It is important to understand the bit by bit erosion of any pretense of equity. Patchwork amendment is larded atop patchwork amendment until the entire statute approaches a ridiculous complexity. Yet each piece of legislation is enacted to the accompaniment of flights of rhetoric and the hope of a just allocation of the cost of government. The end result—perhaps the inevitable result given the nature of our society—is one unholy rip-off.

11

Where Is the Money Coming From?

A wise man once said, "Show me your tax system and I'll tell you about your country."

The author has attempted to show the reader the American tax system. It is now for the reader to judge whether the system merits the characterization of Henry George,

> Our revenue laws as a body might well be entitled "Acts to promote the corruption of public officials, to suppress honesty and encourage fraud, to set a premium upon perjury and the subornation of perjury and to divorce the idea of law from the idea of justice."

Perhaps Theodore White was correct, perhaps George McGovern exceeded the speed limit of change and went around the bend too fast. Perhaps Mr. McGovern suffered from sloppy arithmetic and grandiose overstatement, but he nevertheless took aim at the right target—the gross maldistribution of income and wealth that may well be the fundamental American problem.

But the seeds have been sown, the doubts have been raised. The cries to take the rich off welfare will grow louder. An idea whose time has come cannot be muted indefinitely.

For who can justify the concept that "money made by money" should not be taxed at the same rate as money made by men? As Robert K. Lipton, who coined the phrase, explains, "My phrase lingers on, not because it is catchy, but because of the inexorable logic of the underlying concept."

Neither economic policy nor fairness warrants different tax treatments for the fruits of capital against the fruits of labor. There is no reason to provide greater rewards and incentives to the person who puts his money in the stock market than to the person who deposits it in a commercial bank or savings institution, which in turn lends it or invests it in American industry. Why should the people who spend their efforts on activities like creating entrepreneurial investments, or studying and investing in stocks or real estate enjoy a lower tax on the return from their work product than those who manage our government and our business, care for our health, create our arts, or otherwise provide the labor that keeps our country functioning?

How do the activities that generate this unearned income add to the supply of goods and services available to society? Is the unearned income a result of the efforts of its recipient or is the recipient merely reaping the benefit of the exertions of others?

How much longer will we put up with welfare for the rich? True, we agree with Peter Barnes that rich people's welfare has many advantages over welfare for the poor. There is no legal ceiling, no humiliating means test, no prying by social workers, no questions about men living in the house, no public approbrium, no danger of cut-off. The rich can hire accountants, lawyers, and lobbyists to do their chiseling, while they sleep late in the morning and need not worry about the rush hour traffic. But how does all this square with Mr. Nixon's and Mr. Ford's work ethic?

Adlai Stevenson once stated that the American faith has been a faith in a just distribution of the wealth among all of our citizens. He set forth the major belief "the people are all that is important, and that all people are equally important, and that such ideas as property and corporate business are only means, not ends."

If that is so and if tax reform is inexorably logical, just, and a matter of faith and belief, why is it not possible to speedily reform our tax laws? John Gardner of the Urban Coalition provides the answer. It is because the tax system has become enmeshed in an "impenetrable web of vested interests."

Even the entrenched bureaucracy of the Internal Revenue Service is seeking to perpetuate itself by setting up a special services staff to investigate so-called "tax rebels", who are defined as "tax resistance organizations and those individuals who publicly advocate non-compliance with the tax laws."

Thus, most experts see little prospect of early reform. Joseph A. Pechman and George F. Breale wrote a book entitled *Federal Tax Reform. The Impossible Dream?* To expect otherwise is the height of naivété. A colossal historical inequity like the American tax structure, a mechanism subtly fastened, as we have seen, on a people with a view towards extracting from them that produce of their labor not absolutely necessary for subsistence, is not easily removed. The tax structure is an essential element of a society that has been fashioned over the course of two centuries in a specific way in order to serve the interests of designated hereditary beneficiaries and their retainers and emulators.

It is even doubtful that such an upheaval of the social system, as true tax reform would entail, could be accomplished by means of elections or the passage of laws. We did not need the Nixon administration to demonstrate that the arrangements under which popular elections have been held and laws passed since the birth of our Republic have been as crooked as a fixed wheel in a low gambling joint. Nor are great currents of history reversed by small laws.

It is doubtful further that this reform can be accomplished by any means short of revolution, and it is just this inequality of treatment under the tax laws that may provide the spark. Professor Robert Nesbit of the University of Arizona writes,

> All revolutions in history have originated in perceptions of inequity, not, as is more commonly believed, in loss of individual freedom. Any power can and generally will be endured if only it is thought to affect all people equally.

Only twice since its inception in 1913 has the federal tax structure been revised. And these two revisions—in 1939 and 1954—were, according to a former Commissioner of Internal Revenue, only "facelifting." The Tax Reform Acts of 1969 and 1976, as we have seen, provided little reform and even this bit was nullified by the 1971 act. Just whisper tax reform and the lobbyists and special pleaders descend on Washington like locusts. For every loophole that is plugged, ingenious tax lawyers open two new ones. A Congressman once tried to explain, "I write a law. You drill a hole in it. I plug the hole. You drill a hole in my plug." Old loopholes never die; they become larger. Randolph Paul likened them to guests who come to dinner and refuse to go home.

That is why this book began with a plea to the one percent of the population who owns America. It is axiomatic that those who suffer most from ill-designed economic institutions have the least power to effect change, whereas those who have the power are little inclined to correct or even to question a system that favors them. It is the purpose of this book to arouse those who have the power to their perils, their obligations, and their challenge. For, in the final analysis, it falls to the rich to provide for the social needs of their less-fortunate fellow citizens. The first move, the initiative, toward the creation of a socially just America must come from the rich.

The national agenda of America contains a good deal of unfinished business that gnaws at our conscience. There are poor to be lifted up, hungry to be fed, sick to be cured, aged to be comforted, children to be taught, the ill-housed to be sheltered, cities to be rebuilt, waters to be purified, airs to be cleansed, a planet to be restored.

In 1944 Franklin Delano Roosevelt proposed a Second Bill of Rights. It was intended not as a law but as a moral commitment for our legislators, our leaders, for our people throughout this, the richest country in the history of the world. This second Bill was to establish a new basis of security and prosperity for all—regardless of station, race, or creed. Among these rights were:

1—The right to a useful and remunerative job in the industries or shops or farms or mines of the Nation;

2—The right to earn enough to provide adequate food and clothing and recreation;

3—The right of every farmer to raise and sell his products at a return which will give him and his family a decent living;

4—The right of every businessman, large and small, to trade in an atmosphere of freedom from unfair competition and domination by monopolies at home or abroad;

5—The right of every family to a decent home;

6—The right to adequate medical care and the opportunity to achieve and enjoy good health;

7—The right to adequate protection from the economic fears of old age, sickness, accident and unemployment;

8—The right to a good education.

Today, the attainment of these rights seems as far away as ever. If human life is to have meaning, we must elevate it by cleansing it from fear and hatred, slums, ghettos, hunger, ignorance, and disease.

Following the devastating 1967 riots, the Kerner Commission urged a "commitment of national action-compassionate, massive and sustained." That commitment, as well, still awaits implementation.

These are great enterprises we are discussing: to provide for the human needs of our people, to provide a social minimum for each citizen and to restore the social balance that we have allowed to become lopsided.

The Kerner Commission spoke of "unprecedented levels of funding." We have discussed in some detail above the vast sums of money required to right the ills afflicting our society. They run into tens of billions of dollars.

Andrew F. Brimmer, then a member of the Federal Reserve Board, in a commencement address at Middlebury, Vermont, in May 1972, declared that it may be necessary to "raise the average level of taxation in the United States" over the next few years to meet the demands for more public services and to avoid a "serious deterioration" in those services at the state and local level. He stated that over the years ahead there will be no large sum of money that the Government can easily devote to the expansion and improvement of public services, "because the growth of revenues has already been mortgaged."

A similar conclusion had been reached by the Brookings Institution in a study entitled, *Setting National Priorities: The 1973 Budget.* The Brookings budget book found that the Federal Government had already "overcommitted" for the next two years all the revenues it can expect from a growing economy and cannot spend more in the decade ahead on solving social or other problems without a big tax increase.

Where is the money coming from? There are five alternatives:

1—Increase the present tax rates;
2—Reform the tax laws and close the loopholes;
3—Reorder our priorities for Government spending;
4—Industrial expansion;
5—Find new sources of revenue.

Present tax rates are already close to being confiscatory. The *Wall Street Journal* talks about a "rising anger about high taxes of all sorts." There is little doubt that United States taxpayers, who are among the most compliant in the world, are in near revolt against a system that practically no one still defends.

The fat cats can be pushed just so far and the middle class is already bubbling with threats of tax strikes. It was the opinion of Colin Clark, an eminent Australian economist, that a twenty-five percent rate approaches the danger point in income taxes. Even under a no loopholes tax structure, which would make possible an across the board cut of forty-three percent, the tax rates, according to Drs. Pechman and Okner, would still range from seven to forty-four percent instead of the present fourteen to seventy percent.

We have already discussed the dim prospects for reforming the tax laws and closing the loopholes.

Dr. Glenn Seaborg, the codiscoverer of plutonium, in testimony before the House Select Subcommittee on Education, asked that "we sit back and rethink our values, reconsider our activities in terms of the quality of our lives and the directions they were taking." In worshiping the mammon of GNP—gross national product—we give equal weight to napalm and diesel fuel, bombs and bread, defoliates for destroying crops of impoverished Vietnamese and fertilizers, guerrilla warfare training camps and day care centers, distant early warning systems that are obsolete before they are built and garbage processing plants, orbiting space stations and hospitals.

The Rev. Dr. Martin Luther King, Jr., stated, "It is much more important to put men on their own two feet on earth than to put men on the moon."

Our national priorities are certainly distorted when each year the Federal Government spends more than seventy cents of every budget dollar on past, present, and future wars. We devote more resources to the war machine than is spent by all levels of government on health and hospitals, education, old-age and retirement benefits, public assistance and relief, unemployment and social security, housing and community development, and the support of agriculture. Out of every tax dollar there is only about eleven cents left to build American society.

The total cost of armaments and armed forces to the United States since World War II through 1969, estimated at more than one trillion dollars, would have been sufficient to pay for all of the following: a $20,000 house for all families living at the poverty level; a $50 million university for each city with a population of 500,000; a $10 million library for each of these cities; a $3,000 automobile for every family; medical expenses of up to $1,000 for every family for ten years; the salaries of 100,000 teachers at $10,000 per year for one-hundred years; the salaries of 100,000 nurses at $10,000 per year for one-hundred years; the salaries of 100,000 farm workers at $10,000 per year for one-hundred years; and a free college education for every boy and girl between the ages of seventeen and twenty-one. Or, in the alternative, the total cost of armaments would provide a $10,000 income for each family at the poverty level for ten years.

Let us stop daydreaming. We must be realistic. This author has written enough on the subject of disarmament to know how impossible it is to cut the military budget under any circumstances, certainly for the foreseeable future. The total sums involved in nondefense programs are too small to promise any substantial diversion for human needs.

In an article entitled *Don't Knock the $2 Trillion Economy* appearing in the 5 March 1973 *New York Times Magazine,* Columbia University professors Peter Passell and Leonard Ross stated, "Quite simply, growth is the only way in which America will ever reduce poverty." In other words, expand the economy so that we have a larger pie and then each person's slice will be larger.

If the two learned professors are correct, how does one explain away the unacceptable residue of poverty left behind, despite the phenomenal prodigious economic growth of the United States in the twentieth century? In fact, James D. Smith of Pennsylvania State University found that the disparities between the richest and the poorest are widening year by year. To quote Henry George, "The association of poverty with progress is the great enigma of our times."

Professors Barry R. Chiswick and Jacob Mincer project that income distribution in 1985 will be about the same as in 1965. A study by Lester C. Thurow and Robert E.B. Lucas of the Massachusetts Institute of Technology concludes that "future trends in the distribution of income are apt to mirror the trends of the post-war period." We collide with Pareto's Law that an immutable pattern of income inequity is built into the economic system as it is now constituted.

We must conclude that the theory of growth to meet the rising expectations of the poor is a cop-out, a way of avoiding the real social and moral issue of equality. It postpones the day of reckoning to the distant future because it takes a long time to realize the fruits of growth. By then, the poor and we will be dead. The growth theory amounts to answering the poor with voices so sweet, "Course you'll eat bye and bye, in the glorious land above the sky; work and pray, live on hay, you'll get pie in the sky when you die."

Of course, there are those who regard growth as a terminal disease but that is another story.

We have thus pretty well demolished four of the five alternatives to the question: Where is the money coming from? The only resource left to us is to find new sources of revenue.

President Nixon proposed a value-added tax-in effect, a national sales tax. But this proposal was widely criticized as a regressive measure and a Gallup poll found that fifty-one percent of those interviewed opposed such a tax.

What then?

12

A Tax on Wealth

At first blush, such a quest for new sources of revenue seems downright silly. We all know that everything possible is now taxed with the exception of the air we breathe, and it will not be long before the government puts a meter on that, too. Further, we have to make certain that any new source of revenue meets the test of not being regressive and is levied according to the ability to pay.

The modern principle of taxation as set forth by Adam Smith bears repeating:

> The subject of every state ought to contribute towards the support of the government, as nearly as possible, in proportion to their respective abilities; that is, in proportion to the revenue which they respectively enjoy under the protection of the State.

With this standard in mind, there are any number of books that weigh the American system in the balances and find it wanting. Many an author has bewailed the inequities of taxation and delineated in precise detail the obstacles that stand in the way of achieving a fair distribution of the burden of government support. But to the knowledge of the author, no scholar has come forth with a workable solution to the crucial issue of inequity in taxation, income, and wealth. Ultimately, each learned tome is absent of a remedy.

Let us look at the Adam Smith criteria again. The key words are "in proportion to their respective abilities" and "in proportion to the revenue."

But is there not another test of the respective ability to pay taxes? Why limit taxes in proportion to the revenue, or income? Is it not the wealth we respectively enjoy under the protection of the state an equally good, or better measure of our ability to pay?

A works as a typist and receives a salary of $5,500 a year. B has deposited $100,000 in a savings bank and receives $5,500 a year in interest. Who has the greater ability to pay taxes? Who has the greater taxable capacity? Yet, the law draws an iron curtain between revenue (or income) and capital (or wealth). Income is taxed; wealth is ignored as if it never existed.

It is all a reflection of the cloak of sanctity that has been thrown around wealth—wealth the unmentionable, the ineffable. Perhaps that is the reason why there has been so little discussion of wealth taxes compared to other sources of revenue in the United States.

This writer knows of only one serious book that deals with the subject. That book is *Taxation of Personal Wealth* by Alan A. Tait published in 1967 by the University of Illinois Press. Since Mr. Tait is a lecturer and tutor at Trinity College, Dublin University, Ireland, it is understandable that his work is addressed principally towards British readers. Diogenes, in his book *The April Game: Secrets of an Internal Revenue Agent,* published in 1973 by the Playboy Press, devotes a small section to a wealth tax. In 1963 there was one article by A.T. Peacock in the *British Tax Review* on the subject and one by M. Stewart in *Bankers Magazine.* Peter Barnes made a passing reference to an annual wealth tax in a 1972 article in the New Republic.

That is about the sum total of bibliography on the subject of wealth taxation appearing the last decade or so. Yet, the concept of a wealth tax is as old as civilization itself. Solon, in ancient Athens, introduced the idea of a net-wealth tax under which each citizen was supposed to pay according to how much property he owned. Ancient Rome, and England and Ireland during the Middle Ages levied wealth taxes that were assessed in accordance with wealth clues, such as, the number of horses, or slaves, or windows, or chimneys.

In modern times, many countries have experimented with the net-worth tax. The outstanding example is India but this form of tax has also been tried in Japan, Nicaragua, the Scandinavian countries, the cantons of Switzerland, the Netherlands, and Sri Lanka. The Organization of American States 1962 Santiago, Chile conference on fiscal policy for economic growth in Latin America recommended a net-worth tax. The European Economic Community Fiscal and Financial Committee, in the 1963 Neumark Committee report on tax harmonization, proposed the study of the general taxation of wealth as a complement to the personal income tax. The British Labor Government in April 1975 proposed an annual charge on personal wealth of more than £100,000 at rates ranging from one to five percent.

But our minds have become so accustomed (or brainwashed) to regarding income as the conventional definition of the measure of taxable capacity that it requires an effort of imagination, a wrench of intellect, to grasp the new concept of wealth as an additional yardstick.

For instance, even Michael Harrington, in testimony before the Joint Economic Committee of Congress, advocated doing away "with all other taxes, federal, state and local, to rely upon a really progressive income tax as the sole source of public funds for all purposes." The AFL-CIO Executive Council at its winter 1973 meeting issued a major statement on taxation entitled *The Goal is Tax Justice*, but confined itself to remedying the abuses of the income tax.

In our example of A and B above, who would be more likely to go out and buy a new spring outfit without first hesitating and counting her pennies, A or B? Wealth provides reserve spending power. Would you argue that A is as well off as B because she earns as much? The maintenance of living standards by continued spending out of capital is a far more important feature among persons with accumulated funds than among those with modest resources. If the theory of taxation based on ability to pay is grounded on a minimum of aggregate sacrifice or equiproportionate sacrifice derived from the law of diminishing marginal utility, who suffers the greater sacrifice when she pays her taxes, A or B?

Everyone must see that the consumption of the rich does not bear the same relation to the consumption of the poor as the income of one does to the wages of the other.

Professor W. Hamburger studied the relation of consumption to wealth and the wage rate over the period 1929 to 1950. He found that wealth accounted for over one-half of consumption but for less than one-third of income, suggesting that the marginal and average propensity to consume property income is about three times as high as the propensity to consume labor income.

It thus becomes evident that income, taken by itself, is an inadequate yardstick of taxable capacity. For that matter, taxable capacity cannot be adequately measured either by income alone or by capital wealth alone. Nicholas Kaldor tells us that a separate tax on each, income and capital, provides jointly a better measure of taxable capacity than either form of taxation taken by itself. Income and wealth taxes complement and reinforce each other. The combination of both of these taxes provides for a much better-balanced tax system than one concentrating on income alone.

Further, income taxes are slanted in favor of those who made their fortunes either before the passage of the Sixteenth Amendment, or before tax rates became progressive. High taxation of current money income fossilizes the existing inequities of wealth. It makes the charmed circle of the already rich that much more charmed because admittance to the circle becomes increasingly less attainable. It discriminates against the Horatio Alger who is trying to make his way up the ladder.

A wealth tax, in combination with an income tax, serves other purposes. After all, the tax burden borne by Americans is lower than that borne in any other industrialized country, except Switzerland and Japan, each of which has a far smaller military establishment than the other countries. According to figures published by the Organization for Economic Cooperation and Development, taxes collected in the United States amounted to 27.9 percent of the gross national product, e.g. the total output of goods and services.

The highest tax burden was in Sweden, with forty-three percent, followed, among others, by Netherlands with 39.7 percent, Denmark with 38.7 percent, Norway with 38.4 percent, the United Kingdom with 36.8 percent, France with 36.3 percent, Austria with 35.6 percent, West Germany with 34.0 percent, Belgium with 33.8 percent, Canada with 30.2 percent, and Italy with 30.1 percent. The percentages for Japan and Switzerland were 19.4 percent and 21.5 percent respectively.

However, only in four nations do individual taxpayers pay a larger share in the form of personal income taxes. In the United States, they represent 34.4 percent of the total tax collections. In Sweden, it is 44.1 percent, Denmark 42.5 percent, Switzerland 36.6 percent, and Australia 36.1 percent. In all other nations, taxpayers pay a smaller share of their total taxes in the form of income taxes.

United States corporations also pay a larger share of their total taxes in the form of taxes on profits than do corporations in most other lands. Compared with 13.7 percentage here, corporations in only three other countries pay more; Japan with 20.3 percent, Australia with 15 percent, and Luxembourg with 14.2 percent.

Thus, where steeper progression is desired on income

taxes, the wealth tax serves as a means of topping off the tax structure. For example, the Shoup mission to Japan in 1949 found that,

> The most satisfactory solution to the problem posed here (the impossibility under the circumstances of pushing income tax rates beyond 50 per cent) involves the imposition of an annual, low rate tax on the net worth of well-to-do individuals . . . so that it would take effect only when the income tax rate schedule levels off. . . . .Such a net worth tax would not be subject to most of the difficulties that militate against the retention of high rates of income tax.

The wealth tax would prove a beginning towards moderating the lopsided distribution of wealth that was detailed earlier in this book. As a matter of fact, wealth is distributed much more unevenly than income. Thus, the richest ten percent of the population receive twenty-nine percent of personal income, but own fifty-six percent of the national wealth, while the poorest ten percent receive one percent of the income and are in debt to boot. In fact, a full twenty-five percent of the population is unable to report any net worth at all.

At the top of the wealth distribution, one percent of the wealth holders own twenty-five percent of all the physical and financial wealth, and possess upwards of seventy percent of all productive capital. At the same time, this one percent now contributes only fourteen percent of all taxes.

It is estimated that a redistribution of only five percent of the national income could bring every family in America up to a minimum income of $5,000 per annum. A word of caution is due here. We do not want to fall into the "arithmetic of happiness" trap so eloquently explained by Bertrand de Jouvenal in his *The Ethics of Redistribution.* We should be aware that the calculations by redistributionists on what has to be taken from whom never seem to work out and the end result is the more redistribution the more power to the State.

Let us define our terms.

A net worth or wealth tax is a direct tax imposed on individuals, corporations, or other entities on the basis of the total worth of each on a net basis, that is, net of all outstanding liabilities. The wealth tax is a regular, recurring annual tax, imposed on a graduated scale, on the net worth of the reporting entity as of the end of the reporting period. Theoretically, the incidence of such a tax should fall directly on the taxpayer and cannot readily be shifted.

We are not referring to in rem or property taxes, such as real property taxes, or intangible property taxes, which are imposed on the gross value of the asset without deduction for liabilities, such as mortgages. Thus, a wealth tax is fairer because it takes debt into consideration.

Nor are we referring to noncurrent capital levies that are usually one-time impositions. By their nature, these are emergency taxes levied under extraordinary circumstances. Thus, West Germany, in order to equalize the burden of postwar reconstruction enacted the Lastenausgleichsvermögensabgable saddling all property owned as of 21 June 1948 with a fifty percent tax with installment payments permitted over a thirty-year period beginning 1 April 1949.

As we can readily surmise, a capital levy is a substitute for borrowing and is preferable to transfer of national wealth to the rich in the form of bonds. David Ricardo had proposed that England retire its huge debt at the close of the Napoleonic Wars by a special levy on capital. John Stuart Mill had looked with favor on this proposal. Germany had levied an emergency capital tax in 1918 at the close of World War I.

Similar levies have been imposed, on various occasions, by Hungary, Czechoslovakia, Finland, the Netherlands, Britain, Denmark, and Austria. During the course of World War II Sir Maynard Keynes, in *How to Pay for The War,* called for a capital levy.

By adopting a net-wealth tax, whole new dimensions and horizons of vast sources of revenue are opened.

As we noted above, there are no official comprehensive estimates of the national wealth. You will search in vain through the usual household almanacs—the World Almanac, the Information Please Almanac, the New York Times Encyclopedia Almanac, or the Readers Digest Almanac and Yearbook—for statistics on national wealth. The Statistical Abstract of the United States sets the total tangible assets for 1968 at $3.0794 trillion, as follows:

Structures		$1,5370	trillion
Equipment	producer durables	.3770	
	consumer durables	.2338	
Inventories		.2162	
Land		.7154	
	Total	$3.0794	

But the table does not include cash and other intangibles.

Raymond W. Goldsmith in a 1952 study for the National Bureau of Economic Research estimated the total wealth of all sectors at $2,3393 trillion and the total wealth in the personal sector at $1,1048 trillion. For that year total wealth was 7.1 times the 1951 gross national product of $329.822 billion.

John W. Kendrick, in an article entitled *The Wealth of the United States,* appearing in the January 1967 issue *Finance,* estimated the net worth of the nation at $2.460 trillion, as follows:

Tangible assets	$2.390	trillion
Financial Assets	2.220	
Net foreign assets	.020	
Total	$4.630	
Liabilities	2.170	
Net Worth	$2.460	

The February 1967 issue of that magazine estimated the total net worth of corporations at $371 billion.

James D. Smith estimated the net worth of the personal sector at four trillion dollars at the beginning of 1972, up from three trillion dollars in 1968. The National Commission on Urban Problems, chaired by Paul Douglas, estimated that land values had risen an average of twenty-five billion dollars a year during the 1960s. Lewis Mandell of the University of Michigan Survey Research Center is of the opinion that the national wealth has doubled since 1953.

Based upon these studies, a current estimate of national net worth of five trillion dollars would appear reasonably conservative. Thus a nominal tax of one percent would yield fifty billion dollars in new, and almost painless, revenue. In practice, however, a new wealth tax would carry a graduated rate schedule. Thus, when we keep in mind United States Treasury statistics that in 1962 the total wealth of the richest two percent of the population was greater than the gross national product, the yield from a wealth tax could conceivably yield a great deal more than fifty billion dollars.

The inheritance tax, in principal, has been hailed as "one of the best, fairest, most easily borne that political economists have yet discovered as applicable to modern society." Why should not the same argument, in principle, hold true for the wealth tax?

Given a wealth tax, we can begin to answer that momentous question: What is the purpose of all the American wealth? We can, in some small measure, stop the runaway abuse of our nation's wealth and turn it to use to make life a bit more tolerable for our less-fortunate fellow men. We may then begin to realize that taxes can do a great deal more than raise revenues. The power to tax need not be the power to destroy; it may be the power to fulfill.

Dr. Philip M. Hauser, president of the National Conference on Social Welfare, declared, "We must come to recognize that the welfare of the poor and the handicapped is at least as important as the welfare of the Pennsylvania Railroad, Lockheed, ITT, milk trusts, agribusiness, and oil companies, to mention a few."

In addition to taxing the wealth accumulations of individuals and business entities, there is no reason why the new wealth tax should not be levied against other repositories of great wealth such as churches, foundations, pension plans, etc. The property of these sanctuaries from taxation also enjoy the protection of the State and they should bear a fair share of the cost.

At one time it may have been argued that the State should exempt religious institutions from taxation as an adjunct of its more direct police powers because religion made people more readily tractable. Present crime rates belie this argument. Let the church, therefore, render unto Caesar what is Caesar's.

James Gollin, in his book *Worldly Goods,* estimates the total wealth of the American Catholic Church at $34.2 billion in 1971. In January 1972, the National Council of Churches submitted a report stating that the nation's three major religions had about $22 billion invested in the stock market. Martin Larson, in an article entitled *Church Wealth and Business Income* appearing in the October 1964 issue of *Church and State,* set the value of all church property in the United States at $80 billion. Writing in his book *The Great Tax Fraud,* in 1968, he increased his valuation of church holdings to $200 billion.

Add to the potential source of revenue from a wealth tax more than $25 billion in assets held by foundations. The 1971 Foundation Directory puts the asset value of the Ford Foundation alone at $2.902 billion, followed by the Robert Wood Johnson Foundation with $1.200 billion, the Lilly Endowment with $778 million, the Rockefeller Foundation with $757 million, and the Andrew W. Mellon Foundation with $697 million.

A Congressional labor subcommittee estimated in February 1972 that private pension plans had approximately $135 billion in assets and investments, and that this amount was growing by $10 billion annually. By 1975, they amounted to $160 billion.

Nearly one-third of all real estate in the United States is tax exempt, although very often the real estate is being used for investment instead of the purposes for which the organization was established. If we include with the above churches, foundations, and pension funds other tax exempt entities such as schools, cemeteries, eleemosynary institutions, cultural institutions, professional associations, clubs, historical and literary societies, and other now-exempt organizations, we would restore millions of dollars in wealth to the tax rolls.

"Well and good," our critics will say, "You make a case for a wealth tax, but will it stand up? Is it Constitutional?"

It is the opinion of the author that a wealth tax is well within the purview of Congressional authority under the Constitution.

It is a well-established principle of the common law that the whole of private property and the income derived therefrom is a gift from the community. It is only by the will of the community, as given expression by the State and its government, that particular individuals can enjoy the privileges of ownership protected by the law and by the administrative agencies created by law. Thus, property is a legal concept, and property rights exist only as defined and enforced by governments.

The original distribution of property, often on some basis no longer socially acceptable such as, expropriation by force, exploitation of child labor or bucket-shop stock swindling, is codified, legalized and guaranteed by the power of the law. That which the law grants, the law has the power to limit within Constitutional perimeters.

In fact, the colonies addressed themselves to this very problem immediately after the American revolution. Under the old world rules of inheritance, estates descended to the heirs under the rules of primogeniture and entail. Thus, the male firstborn would inherit the entire estate and the property could be held in perpetuity.

In order to ensure the breakup of the large landed estates and to rescue them from *mortmain*—the clutch of the dead hand—each of the colonies (now states), beginning with North Carolina and Massachusetts in 1784, adopted laws abolishing primogeniture and entail. The preamble to the Maryland law reads as follows: "Whereas, the law of descents which originated with the feudal system and military tenures is contrary to justice and ought to be abolished . . ."

One of the first taxes levied by the colonies was the faculty tax. Thus, New Plymouth in 1643 levied a tax on its colonists "according to their estates or faculties, that is, according to goods, lands, improved facilites and personal abilities." By the time of the Revolutionary War, more than one-third of the colonies had a faculty tax. South Carolina and Massachusetts did not repeal theirs until the Civil War.

Everyone is familiar with the real-estate tax. Real property, personal property, and intangibles have been subject to taxation since time immemorial.

Yes, the critics will say, all true, but you are talking about state and municipal taxes, while the wealth tax you propose is a Federal tax.

Yes, but we have discussed earlier Federal taxes on wealth in the form of stamp and inheritance taxes. The current Federal inheritance tax dates back to 1916, and its constitutionality is now accepted without question. We also have Federal gift taxes that, except for some time gaps, go back to the Revenue Act of 1924. Certainly, these are Federal taxes on property.

Blackstone stated in his *Commentaries on the Laws of England* that, "naturally speaking, the instant a man ceases to be, he ceases to have any dominion." It is the law that permits the property to be transmitted unto the heirs and that spells out the successive rights of generations to inherit the fortunes of previous generations. What the law permits, it can, and has, limited. Certainly, gift and inheritance taxes are limits on the free possession of property. Other laws, such as the Securities and Exchange Act, limit the uses of property.

Probably never in history has a property owner held his possessions as inviolably his own, to do with as he pleases and to bequeath as he pleases without diminution.

In a sense, an estate tax is a levy upon the winnings in a birth lottery. At the present time, the estate tax reaches only one decedent out of one hundred. Theoretically, the Congress now has the authority to tax every estate and to push the rate up to the point where it becomes totally confiscatory.

Is there any difference between an estate tax and a wealth tax except for the point of time at which it is levied?

Estimated taxes are very popular now. Individuals pay estimated taxes on next year's income tax. Corporations pay estimates on their next year's corporation income tax. The rationale behind gift taxes is that they are estimates against the ultimate inheritance tax. That is why gift taxes are calculated on the accumulated gifts made over the years. The lower differential rate for gift taxes were justified as a rough approximation of the compound rate of interest that the property would have earned if held to death.

Why then can we not consider an annual wealth tax as an anticipatory tax, an estimated tax paid each year against the inheritance tax that our estate will owe on death? If the income tax is prepaid in periodic quarterly installments, why cannot the inheritance tax be prepaid in periodic annual installments? It becomes a question of semantics. Is a wealth tax more Constitutional if we term it an estimated inheritance tax?

13

The Mechanics of a Wealth Tax

How would an annual net-worth tax work in practice?

Let us look at the Swedish förmögenhetsshatt. A fully integrated form, giving the data required for both the income tax and the net-wealth tax, is required to be filed annually. Husband and wife, and children under twenty, living at home, file a single return. Although there is an exemption of 150,000 Swedish kroner, everyone must file even if the wealth is less than the exemption or the taxpayer is in debt.

Taxes are levied according to the following rate schedule:

NET PROPERTY VALUE	TAX
Up to 150,000 Swedish kroner	none
150,000 to 250,000 Skr.	1 percent on excess over Skr. 150,000
250,000 to 400,000 Skr.	Skr. 1,000 plus 1.5 percent on excess over Skr. 250,000
400,000 to 1,000,000 Skr.	Skr. 3,250 plus 2 percent on excess over Skr. 400,000
Over 1,000,000 Skr.	Skr. 15,250 plus 2.5 percent on excess over Skr. 1,000,000

But the tax cannot exceed eighty-five percent of that year's income.

Household goods, books, works of art in personal collections, and certain kinds of personal insurance are exempt. Real estate is reported at assessed value. Corporations are exempt.

As we have seen, Sweden bears the highest tax burden in the world. But it is not the type of tax that gives the high ratio of taxation to national product. That ratio is the product of the revenue required to finance the programs of a given country: here, specifically, the cradle-to-the-grave social insurance program of Sweden. Alternate methods might well have been chosen to return the required revenue. For instance, Israel does not have wealth taxes yet bears a very heavy tax load.

How can the Swedish experience with a net-wealth tax be applied to the United States, keeping in mind that Sweden, too, has a self-assessment tax system?

Justice Howell E. Jackson characterized the American tax system as "taxation by confession." On April 15th of each year, millions of citizens voluntarily mail to the Internal Revenue Service Form 1040 detailing the income received during the previous calendar year, itemizing the deductions to which they are entitled, calculating the tax due, and voluntarily remitting a check for the balance.

It would only be a natural extension of the income-tax form to require each taxpayer to also submit a summary of assets, liabilities, and net worth as at the end of the previous year. Corporations and partnerships already submit balance sheets as at the end of the two previous years.

The assessment of any tax begins with a form, so the annual wealth tax will require an annual declaration of net worth. This is not as simple as it sounds.

First, we have to determine who owns what. The Japanese net-worth tax floundered on this shoal.

Too often, the true owner of property is not readily identifiable. How do we establish who owns paper money stuffed in mattresses or safe-deposit boxes? How do we match bearer bonds with their rightful owners? To whom do securities registered in brokerage street names belong? What do we do with real-estate deeds recorded in dummy corporations?

Dozens of other complex questions come to mind. No doubt, similar problems afflicted the beginnings of the income and inheritance taxes. The bulk of the Internal Revenue Code bears witness to the attempts at their resolution.

This writer does not pretend to have the final, definitive answers to all questions. He can only offer his ideas. More knowledgeable experts will have to work out the solutions after a good deal more intensive research than is available now. But the difficulties posed by the prospect of an annual-wealth tax should not detract from the basic, fundamental concept of wealth taxation. That principle is far too important to be sidetracked by technical troubles. Anything worthwhile is only achieved through intensive hard work and effort. Given the will, the problems will be solved.

It is this writer's suggestion that all paper currency be recalled and replaced with new currency, so that the old paper money would not be legal tender after a fixed date. All money exchanged would be accompanied by a record that could be checked against the cash reported by the taxpayer. Other countries, such as Germany, have issued money in new forms, usually as a weapon against the black market. Also, all foreign holdings of bank accounts, cash, stock, real estate, investments, etc., would have to be registered. At present, one must declare all foreign bank accounts.

Bearer and street-registered securities would be outlawed. All nominee holdings would have to be reregistered. Blank transfers of securities through the use of stock powers would no longer be permitted. All evidences of equity and debt will henceforth have to set forth the name of the true holder. As a matter of fact, all property will have to be recorded in the name of or transferred to an identifiable owner. The holding of precious metals would not be permitted in the same way that Americans were not allowed to own gold until 1975.

This writer toyed with the idea of passing a proportionate share of the wealth of corporations through to its stockholders, but rejected the concept as too cumbersome. Probably, a similar problem was faced and similarly resolved by the drafters of the income-tax law. Pension and profit sharing trusts, charitable foundations, labor unions, churches and other voluntary organizations, such as clubs and burial societies, should probably come under the same rules.

All other entities, however, because they ordinarily have few participants, will pass proprietorship through to the beneficial owners. Thus, partnerships, trusts, and estates would have to indicate on their tax reports the ultimate division of the net worth. Where there are life estate beneficiaries and remaindermen, an allocation would have to be made based on actuarial life expectancies. All these calculations, however, would only have to be made once—with the filing of the first return. Subsequently, all percentages will remain the same unless changed, of course, by outside events. With some exceptions, partnerships, trusts, and estates now pass through their income to beneficiaries.

A great body of judicial precedents has already been compiled relating to the ownership of property for inheritance tax purposes. Thus, a Totten trust belongs to the depositor, a life insurance policy belongs to whoever pays the premiums and has the power to change the beneficiary, etc., etc. There is no reason why this body of law cannot carry over to a net-worth tax.

One problem still to be tackled is the division of wealth among the members of a family. One thing is certain: given a graduated tax, wealth will eventually spread itself ratably among the members of a family. The Treasury faced the same situation with regard to family partnerships and finally threw in the sponge. One purpose of our tax program is to make the assessment of taxes as simple as humanly possible. Therefore, it is our suggestion that a family be given the option of filing one joint return covering everyone, children included, or of filing separate returns for each individual. This rule should cover all persons of the household living under one roof and related by blood, marriage, or adoption.

In the next chapter, we shall discuss other taxes that should be included in a tax program for America. If a family chooses a joint form of return, all other returns would also have to be joint. The calculation of the wealth tax on a family joint return would involve dividing the family net worth shown by the number of individuals included. The tax would be calculated on the answer and then remultiplied by the number in the family.

Thus, suppose a family consists of a father, mother, and three children and the net worth comes to $100,000. Dividing this by five gives us a tax basis of $20,000. If the tax at that bracket amounts to $200, that amount times five or $1,000 represents the family's annual-wealth tax.

Agreed, a family tax would yield less revenue but the rates are so small that the revenue loss will not be catastrophic. Besides, reporting of wealth by family is more representative of the true state of affairs.

Now that we have somehow identified who are the owners of wealth, what items of wealth are we concerned with in a wealth tax? Certainly, we do not expect Mr. Taxpayer to list four suits, two pairs of shoes, fourteen sets of underwear, and one wrist watch. Nor do we expect to employ an army of snoopers who will peer into Mrs. Taxpayer's closet to make sure that she does not own a mink coat that is not being reported.

We should only be concerned with significant assets that can be readily traced such as real estate, cash, bank deposits, securities, cash surrender value of life insurance, interests in estates and trusts, mortgages, notes and other receivables, precious metals, business assets, foreign holdings, other investments as in joint ventures, and the like.

We should not be concerned with personal effects such as clothing, or appliances, or automobiles, or furniture, or ordinary jewelry, or musical instruments, or sporting equipment, or most consumer durables. Such items should be listed in accordance with the insurance in force. A personal property, fine arts, jewelry, fur, or automobile policy should, except for the $10,000 limit mentioned below, be determinative of the value of the assets covered. If the owner elects to take the risk of not insuring such items, then there is no wealth to be reported. Consumer purchases will also be dealt with under the expenditures tax that we will discuss in the next chapter.

However, in order to make sure that Mr. Taxpayer does not bury his treasure in yachts, old masters, or Rolls-Royce autos, a ceiling of perhaps $10,000 should be placed on the purchase of nonbusiness assets. Anything costing over that amount, regardless of insurance coverage, would arbitrarily be classified as an investment asset and, therefore, reportable for wealth-tax purposes.

Thus far, we have tried to identify who owns the wealth and to define the type of wealth with which we are concerned. Now the problem is to put a dollar value on these items of wealth. The Nicaraguan net-worth tax ran into trouble on this score.

There are essentially three standards of valuation of assets: cost, fair market value, and appraised or assessed value.

How and how often will assets be revalued? Retained by India to advise on the establishment of a wealth tax. Nicholas Kaldor suggested that book values be used except for the initial reporting and the happening of certain events, such as death. India rejected this suggestion and provided for annual valuation of assets.

This writer, however, is inclined, in the interests of simplicity, to use cost or book value throughout up to the time of death, gift, or other disposition. The cost or book value is the basis for the asset that the taxpayer would have reported if he had sold the asset. For depreciable property, this would be cost less depreciation allowed or allowable. The use of a cost value is important so that we do not lose the tax on the gain if the asset is sold for a price above cost. Of course, all further acquisitions would also be valued at actual cost.

Remember that we considered the annual net wealth tax an estimate towards the final inheritance tax. Thus, when the taxpayer died, a final wealth tax return would be filed. At that time, it would be necessary to value the assets according to the fair-market value as of the date of death. Rather exhaustive rules for the determination of the value of estates have been established in the administration of the present federal inheritance tax, and there is no reason why these rules cannot be carried over.

The final wealth-tax return would be the equivalent of and serve as a substitute for an inheritance tax return. Having already prepaid to a large extent the inheritance tax by way of annual estimates, the estate will owe a tax only on the difference between the previous cost basis used for the annual net-worth returns, and the market value as set forth on the final return. In addition, a taxable gain would be realized on the difference between the cost of the assets as previously reported and the fair market value at death, and, as detailed in the next chapter, individual inheritances would be subject to a receipts tax on the part of the legatee.

In the reverse, if the asset had gone down in value, a credit would be allowed on the final wealth-tax return and a capital loss would result.

As under 1976 law, the heirs would take the assets at the market-value basis reported for estate-tax purposes. Present gift-tax rules for valuation should be changed, however, to conform to estate tax procedures. Thus, a donee would take at current market value and the donor may have realized gain. Here, too, the donor would adjust the valuation of the gift property to its fair market value on his wealth-tax return for the year of the gift, and the individual recipient would include the gift in calculating his receipts tax.

How will the valuation-reporting operate in practice? The taxpayer will list his assets at cost, subtract his liabilities, and come up with his net worth.

Suppose Mr. Taxpayer buys a painting by Mr. Unknown Artist for $200 and eventually it is worth $50,000; or suppose

Mr. Taxpayer puts together piece by piece a stamp collection that is now worth $50,000. Under our definitions, neither of these assets would be subject to the wealth tax before death as long as they were not covered by insurance. But if they were sold, then the proceeds would come under the receipts tax that will be discussed in the next chapter.

Suppose Mr. Taxpayer buys a $4,000 furniture suite on the installment plan. Since the asset is not reportable except under a blanket insurance policy, may the liability be deducted on the net-worth statement? Evidently. The total of such items should not be that significant and most of the instances will probably occur among taxpayers that will report minus equities in any event.

Who should be required to file net-worth reports and what exemption should be allowed?

It is the feeling of this writer that a net-worth report should be required from everyone even if no tax is due. First, the returns would help toward compiling data of national wealth that are now seriously deficient compared with national income statistics. Second, the net-worth report is vital for facilitating auditing and for enforcement of the tax program outlined in the following chapter. Third, the return would serve as a basis for calculation at a time when the taxpayer becomes liable for a tax. Fourth, it would serve to identify the person filing the report with his government. This identification is achieved only twice a year for the average taxpayer—when he votes and when he files his tax return; and barely 60 percent of the population bothers to vote, even in presidential elections.

It is the further feeling of this writer that no exemption should be allowed in computing the wealth tax. As noted earlier, twenty-five percent of the population would be exempt in any event, because they would not have any net worth to report. Receipts and expenditure taxes, as discussed in the next chapter, would, of necessity, require liberal exemptions. Thus, the wealth tax would remain as the only direct tax to which the great majority of the citizens would be subject.

The absence of an exemption is eminently fair. A citizen holds wealth by virtue of the acquiescence of the State and enjoys the wealth by virtue of the protection of the State. Thus, he owes a peculiar obligation to the State since he derives special advantages from the mere existence of organized government as opposed to anarchy.

The little wealth holder benefits as well as the large wealth holder. Each should pay something for that protection. With steeply graduated tax rates, the tax upon the small wealth holder should be little more than token.

There is no greater incentive towards involving a citizen in the functioning of his government than to require him to contribute to the cost of administration. When he has to pay out his hard-earned cash, no matter how small the sum, he will make sure that the budget returns a dollar's worth of services for each dollar of taxes. This consciousness of public burden is the surest method of insuring a proper interest in efficient government.

Will a wealth tax be a step towards a police state?

No believer in the democratic form of government can fail to deprecate the invasion of privacy in this age of the omniscent computer. There is no question but that the recording on tape of individual wealth would strip away another veil from the sanctity of the individual against governmental spying. The Watergate hearings have demonstrated what little meaning the safeguards in the law against divulging taxpayer information really have. Nevertheless, laws would have to be passed making the wealth information concerning the individual inviolate.

The question will have to be weighed in the balance. Certainly, so much personal information is already on record, including income-tax returns, credit reports (which often give net worth information), property ownership, fingerprints, civil service applications, crime reports, newspaper clippings, F.B.I. and police data banks, passport applications, alien reports, etc., etc., that wealth statistics will add little new.

If anything, publication of such statistics may alert the people to the woefully lopsided distribution of wealth in this country. We should not forget that it was the wealthy classes in Japan, Germany, and Italy, as typified by the zaibatsu, which moved each of these nations into fascism and militarism.

14

A Tax Program for America

No system of taxation can be expected to dispense Solomon-like justice to seventy-four million individual taxpayers. It is a well-nigh impossible task to devise a tax system that is both simple and equitable.

It should be apparent by now that the science of taxation is far from exact. It is a poor, inexact art afflicted with many pressures and shades of contradiction. Thus, we can never expect mathematical accuracy in allocating the tax burden.

Ralph Waldo Emerson said, "Of all debts, men are least willing to pay taxes." Edmund Burke sadly noted, "to tax and to please, no more than to love and to be wise, is not given to men." And David Ricardo remarked that, "taxation in every form presents but a choice of evils."

There is no question but that taxation can be a powerful instrument of social progress, but one must recognize the limitations. It would be sheer self-delusion to expect to make taxation into an engine of social revolution. The noble experiment of gradually building a society that is both free and just through progressive taxation is bound to fail unless we recognize this fact.

We shall therefore, limit our objectives to more modest goals. We shall follow that advice of Nobel economist Wassily Leontief, "Change the tax system. Improve it. Redistribute the burden so that the rich pay a little more and the poor pay a little less." We shall, therefore, limit our program to seeking even-handed tax justice, not tax confiscation.

It makes absolutely no sense to mount a wealth tax on the present rotten income-tax base. It is like putting a Lincoln Continental body on a Model T Ford chassis. The operation of the new tax will soon make starkly apparent the defects of the old income tax. Very often, it is more advisable and less costly, in the long run, to stop tinkering with a hopelessly rundown jalopy and abandon it in favor of a new model.

Keeping in mind that direct taxes are levied on persons and indirect taxes on transactions (such as sales), there are essentially only three bases for direct taxation; income or receipts, expenditures or spendings, and net worth or wealth. A combination of all three direct taxes would seem to be the fairest system of taxation for America. Each is interlocking and self-checking in their reporting and in their workings.

We have already discussed the wealth tax. Except for business income, it is proposed to replace the individual income tax with a receipts tax. The taxpayer would be taxed at progressive rates, on all moneys or property received "from whatever source derived." This would include wages, dividends, interest, capital gains above cost, casualty awards above cost, gifts, annuities above cost, oil royalties, other royalties, rents above costs, fees, commissions, welfare payments, tax refunds, scholarship grants, Social Security benefits, railroad retirement benefits, veteran benefits, unemployment insurance, combat pay, workmen compensation benefits, and any other type of receipt.

All receipts will be taxed the same regardless of the source. The taxpayer will add up all his receipts for the year, everything that gives him an ability to buy things: whether wages, capital gains, gifts, inheritances, welfare payments,

Social Security benefits, or whatever. No deductions would be allowed against the receipts tax except for direct expenses to generate receipts such as outside salesman travel necessary to earn commissions. Personal deductions, such as medical expenses, taxes, charities, alimony, casualty losses, child-care expenses, sick pay, etc. would be barred.

Phillip M. Stern proposed taxing as income the rent equivalent on owned homes. The author rejected this concept as too cumbersome and as a nonmonetary benefit that will not fit into our triad of direct taxes.

An annual exemption should be allowed against receipts equal to the higher budget standard of living for an urban family of four as fixed by the Bureau of Labor Statistics. The amount of the exemption would thus fluctuate from year to year. For 1973, for instance, based upon a $16,000 higher budget standard for a family of four, the individual annual exemption would be $4,000 and the family's a multiple of $4,000 depending upon the number of persons included. As with the wealth tax, the family would have the option of filing individually or as a unit.

This writer considered permitting cumulative annual exemptions beginning with the year of birth that would be carried forward indefinitely to the extent not used, but rejected the proposition as too complicated. If each taxpayer started from scratch, such a plan would be feasible, but it becomes very difficult to operate when some taxpayers are new and others have been reporting for many years. A different exemption system for old and new taxpayers would leave us open to cries of discrimination.

So, the receipts-less-the-exemption would give the amount subject to tax that, multiplied by the rate for that bracket, would provide the amount of the receipts tax.

The system of tax collection would be based on the concept of withholding with all disbursers of wages, dividends, interest, royalties, etc. required to withhold according to a sliding scale. Those not subject to withholding or in higher tax brackets would pay quarterly estimates as at present.

The rate of tax should be relatively low because a receipts tax eliminates all loopholes, and we have already noted that such a step alone would lower the income tax rates by forty-three percent. In addition, the wealth and expenditure taxes would spread the burden.

The last of the triad of taxes is the expenditures tax. This is the third measure of ability to pay. Ogden Mills suggested a spendings taxes as far back as 1921. Two Yale professors of political economy, Irving Fisher and Thomas S. Adams, long favored this type of impost. Henry Morgenthau suggested a spendings tax in 1942, but the Senate Finance Committee rejected it by a vote of twelve to nothing. An editorial in the *New York Times* commented, "no tax proposal ever put forward by the Treasury received such strong and uniform condemnation."

It would be a very simple procedure to calculate the amount of expenditures per year. All that the taxpayer has to do is add receipts to the net worth at the end of the prior year and subtract the current net worth. The answer is the amount of expenditures. It is here that we would pick up lavish expenditures on clothing, jewelry, furs, autos, etc. Such a tax would also act as a brake against heavy spending in the last month in order to show less net wealth as of 1 January.

The exemption for the expenditures tax would be the same as for the receipts tax, namely, the higher-budget standard of living for an urban family of four. Here again, the family would be given the option of choosing between individual and joint returns.

It is acknowledged that the outlawing of all deductions would work severe hardships in instances such as heavy medical bills, funeral expenses, judgments at law, legal fees, casualties, other taxes, and the like, but it was felt that the desirability of simplicity of administration outweighed all the other disadvantages. Furthermore, the expected low rates of tax should ameliorate the hardship inflicted.

The amount of expenditures-less-the-exemption determines the tax base that, multiplied by the rate for the bracket, gives the amount of expenditure tax due.

The receipts and expenditure taxes would apply only to nonbusiness transactions. Corporations and individual proprietors would continue to subtract business costs and expenses from gross income, and pay a tax on net income at the same rate schedule as the receipts tax. Partnerships, trusts, estates, etc., will pass the net income through. Of course, all entities will pay the net-worth tax.

The receipts, expenditures, and wealth taxes would all be reported in and calculated from a single comprehensive tax form. Only one check would go to the Treasury for the quarterly estimates or for the final payment.

Since tax rates are the function of many variables, including the state of the economy and the size of the budget, this writer is in no position to offer a suggested schedule of rates for any of the three imposts. What is feasible today may be out-of-date as of publication as conditions fluctuate. One can only reiterate that the rates must be progressive. Their exact definition is a task for the Congress.

However, the President should have the authority to vary by proclamation the rates of any or all taxes up and down by up to ten percent depending upon economic circumstances. President John F. Kennedy proposed in 1963 that the President be given authority to vary income tax rates as the employment rate and other basic economic indicators went up and down. The proposal did not receive even the courtesy of a Congressional hearing.

It is hoped that, in time, state and municipal budgets will be consolidated with the federal budget so that these three proposed federal taxes will be the only ones levied. The revenues collected could then be shared with the local units.

Every effort has been made to make the tax program for America as simplified and as preference-free as possible. This writer believes that the program is workable. In operation, the three taxes should be self-proving and self-auditing, thus dispensing with the swarm of snoopers with inquisatorial powers that make the NKVD look like house detectives. It should be possible to save a good proportion of the $1.2 billion budget now allotted to the Internal Revenue Service and to transfer most of its bureaucracy of 74,000 employees to more productive work.

It should be mentioned that reform of what Secretary of State William P. Rogers termed the "rotten" system of campaign financing is a precondition of any possible basic tax reform. Campaign funds should be provided by the government to the exclusion of the influence seekers so that money no longer contaminates the political process.

It is an absolute must that the tax program for America also include some system of tax credits to provide a basic income floor for all Americans as a matter of right rather than charity. Every citizen must have the assurance of a decent annual income, although this level should be set to provide a bit less than one could earn by working. Society must provide a safety net to catch even the lowliest members of our nation from crashing to the ground. Income supplements must be provided for our working people who, in spite of their labor, still have difficulty making ends meet.

There should be no doubt left that a negative income tax or guaranteed annual wage would be far superior to our discredited bureaucratic public welfare system, which President Nixon termed a "monstrous consuming outrage, an outrage against the community, against the taxpayer and particularly against the children that it is supposed to help." The era of the Gray Lady Bountiful of the Junior League coming into the slum in all her benevolence to deliver Thanksgiving and Christmas baskets has long passed.

The service concept of mitigating poverty must be replaced by a cycle-breaking self-help approach.

Only some form of income strategy of cash-in-hand stipend, paid out as a matter of right, call it what you will—guaranteed annual income, income security, family assistance plan, income maintenance, negative income tax, or family allowance plan—will wipe out the deceit, corruption, and scars of welfare. This stipend should be paid out as a matter of right with no means test and no questions asked.

Realizing that the old subsidized housing program helped the builders rather than the ill-housed and resulted in scandal, shoddy construction, and profiteering, the Housing and Community Development Act of 1974 provided for direct rent subsidies to tenants. The Federal Government will make up the difference between the actual rent for an apartment and the amount that a family eligible for the program is required to contribute. Family contributions range from fifteen to twenty-five percent of income depending on such factors as family size, location, etc. A family must have annual income that is less than eighty percent of the median in its area ($14,301 in New York City) to be eligible.

The Tax Reduction Act of 1975 for the first time, adopted the principle of the negative income tax. Taxpayers with dependent children will receive a ten percent credit up to a maximum of $400 on earned income. The credit phases out as earnings exceed $4,000, losing $1 of credit for each $10 of income until the credit phases out completely at $8,000. Taxpayers with a credit exceeding their liability get the difference as a refund.

In October 1972, a British government green paper (which never advanced to legislation) proposed a negative income tax under which those with an income level below a certain minimum would receive direct cash payments from the Government. The idea was to raise the incomes of the poor, eliminate the means test, and simplify an admittedly complex and costly welfare administration.

The welfare system should be redefined so that the Government acts as a sort of financial guarantor against illfare. It is the suggestion of this writer that each family of four be guaranteed the annual cost of maintaining a family at the lowest budget level as fixed by the Bureau of Labor Statistics. For 1972, this amount was $7,386.

A family of four reporting less than $7,386 in receipts would receive a direct check from the Treasury. As an incentive for work, a credit of twenty-five percent would be allowed for earned income. Thus, a family would be entitled to some funds until the wage income reached $9,848, or roughly the 1972 median United States household income of $9700.

For example, a family of four with wage income of $8,000, would receive a cash payment of $1,386, a product of $8,000 less twenty-five percent, or $2,000 subtracted from $7,386.

Admittedly, this program would cost vast sums. But we have demonstrated that equally vast sums would become available through the tax on wealth and the elimination of loopholes and subsidies. What we are proposing, however, is such a tremendous step forward that it would not be necessary to institute it to the fullest extent in one fell swoop. The British Government proposed a five-year transition period. It would be a great step forward if our proposal took effect gradually over a five-year or even ten-year period. The present welfare system could be phased out slowly while the negative income tax took over in steps, increasing the direct cash payout year by year.

In seeking the replacement of the present welfare apparatus, we shall encounter the bitter opposition of the existing bureaucracy, of which Daniel P. Moynihan spoke, which consciously or unconsciously benefits from present conditions. But that is the normal reaction facing any society that seeks to press forward.

The negative income tax, however, must be recognized as only one side of the coin. The other side is the rehabilitation of the poor into self-sustaining members of society. Cash payouts to the poor without requiring a sincere, dedicated effort on their part to become economically independent, except where this is impossible because of health, age, or child care reasons, is throwing money to the wind. In Canada, for instance, the family allowance is not paid for school-age children who do not attend school. The result has been a sharp decline in school dropouts.

Danilo Dolci has said that, "Every man has a vast store of riches in his own hands and work." It is the people themselves who are our wealth; it is their brains that are the true gold reserve of the nation. By neglecting the poor, their brains, their labor, and the contribution that they are capable of making we diminish and impoverish our nation. Imagine how our gross national product and the quality of our lives would leap if we restored these millions of persons to productive labor and to the normal responsibilities of citizenship.

Economist Gabriel Hauge has proposed government employment of 500,000 disadvantaged members of the labor force at an annual salary of $7,000 each. Professors William Fellner of Yale and James O'Toole of Southern California have made similar proposals. There is plenty of work that needs to be done. The Employment Act of 1946 mandates the creation of those jobs, and our society will be the better because of them.

The transition period of which we speak affords us a wonderful opportunity to remedy this neglect of our under-employed and to ready our disaffected for their role in society. We must recognize that we have in our midst, a devastated, underdeveloped nation, struggling for its place in the sun. At the end of World War II, Secretary of State George C. Marshall, recognizing that the nations of Europe were devastated and struggling for their place in the sun, made a famous speech at a Harvard commencement.

General Marshall stated that in view of the,

> dislocation of the entire fabric of the European economy, it is logical that the United States do whatever it is able to do to assist in the return of normal economic health in the world, without which there can be no stability and no assured peace.

The United States spent approximately $17 billion under the Marshall Plan to revive the European economy. The results are a spectacular show place of affluence that is the marvel of the world.

We have also extended massive aid to our Latin American neighbors through the Alliance for Progress and to our allies in the Far and Middle East. Can we, in good conscience, do any less for our economically underdeveloped neighbors at home?

Poverty is expensive to maintain. An Alliance for Progress or a Marshall Plan at home would reap a rich harvest in productivity for America and, at the same time, arrest the deterioration of our cities and save untold sums in welfare, police, hospital, and similar appropriations. Similar rehabilitative measures had been proposed in the Whitney M. Young Domestic Marshall Plan, the A. Philip Randolph Freedom Budget, the Martin Luther King Economic Bill of Rights, and by Gunnar Myrdal. The result would be a great living program of human renewal in our land.

Our attack on poverty should be guided by the precept set forth by the ancient sage Maimonides:

> Anticipate charity by preventing poverty; assist the reduced fellow man either by a considerable gift, or a sum of money, or by teaching him a trade, or by putting him in the way of business so that he may earn an honest livelihood and not be forced to the dreadful alternative of holding out his hand for charity.

The key to the attack on poverty is the word "underdeveloped." The underdeveloped lack either capital or know-how or both. Europe had the know-how; it lacked capital. The United States is blessed with capital but our poor lack the know-how. This latter ingredient is the far more difficult to supply. The McCone Commission report on the Watts uprising seemed most surprised by the findings of the education study that showed that the schools in Watts were turning out "social illiterates" and that substantial numbers of black pupils were still unable to read by the end of elementary school.

There is an Oriental proverb that states, "Give a man a fish and he will eat for a day; teach him how to fish and he will eat for the rest of his life." To spread education is to spread prosperity. J.K. Galbraith said, "To the best of my knowledge, there is no place in the world where well-educated people are really poor." Professor Galbraith termed education "the most effective single step that would be taken in the attack on poverty." Education is synonymous with upward mobility in an open society—the only valid passport out of poverty. The lack of education is economic suicide. The Niagara resolutions of the National Association for the Advancement of Colored People declared, "Either the United States will destroy ignorance or ignorance will destroy the United States."

What does it avail the poor if they are gaining legally but falling behind economically? Unskilled jobs are being wiped out by the machine at the same time that they are not acquiring the skills of a modern computerized society.

Arthur Adler, the great psychologist, wrote,

> Whatever name we give it, we shall always find in human beings this great line of activity—the struggle to rise from an inferior position to a superior position, from defeat to victory, from below to above. It begins in our earliest childhood, it continues to the end of our lives.

We must invest more than proportionately in the children of the poor community. It is there that high quality schools, strong health services, and special provisions for nutrition and recreation are most needed. Compensatory education remains the best hope for the children of Appalachia and of the ghetto.

The finest teachers and the finest schools possible must be poured into the nation's poorest counties and the city slums. Intensive aid must be provided in the form of counseling, job coaching, remedial education, vocational training, and follow-up services. Such programs of education in skills and vocations will unleash a power more mighty than dollars. They will enable each American to stretch his talents; they will convert tax eaters into taxpayers.

The program of rehabilitation that we have outlined is much too important to entrust to the tender mercies of indifferent, often hostile, local administrations. A national Development Authority should be organized and funded adequately. It should then be charged with the task of implementing and carrying out the objectives here set forth.

Billions of dollars have been poured into public education since the end of World War II. Yet, we turn out millions of functional illiterates. We have learned the hard way that it is wrong to place the entire burden on the schools, to demand too much from education. Educational policy must be viewed as only one component of a comprehensive social and economic program that addresses itself, in addition, to such pressing social needs as employment, housing, and health care. We know that to improve the academic achievement of the mass of students of our low-income, slum-dwelling families, we have to first permit them to improve their class position, to increase their incomes, and above all, to establish a more stable family life in a more stable and less turbulent neighborhood.

Thus, in addition to rehabilitating the human resources of the nation, the Development Authority must make a beginning towards rebuilding the land. Projects of urban renewal, pollution control, public transportation, and school and hospital construction will provide jobs and training, and at the same time provide for the creation of a decent environment for our children. It is, therefore, a two-prong task that we assign to our Development Authority.

For the present, thank God, the United States is not engaged in any foreign wars. The enemy is here within our borders. If fight we must, the battle lies well within our territory; it is a battle against backwardness and destitution. It is hoped that such a battle would end the tragic human wastage in the slums and among the rural poor, and would provide the present domestic victims of American society with a decent measure of self-respect and happiness. In the words of President Nixon, "Let us begin to turn the blessings of peace into a better life for all."

Perhaps then will we be able to fulfill the promise that is America. Thomas Wolfe expressed that promise most eloquently—

> to every man his chance, to every man regardless of his birth his shining golden opportunity, to every man the right to live and to work and be himself, and to become whatever thing his manhood and his vision can combine to make him. This is the promise of America.

15

Are We Killing the Goose?

It is all very well to outline an euphoric plan on paper. The question is: will it work in practice? If we adopt a wealth tax, if we eliminate tax loopholes and tax gross receipts progressively, if we tax expenditures progressively, if we curtail subsidies and giveaways, if we adopt a negative income tax and institute a domestic Marshall Plan, will we be killing the goose that lays the golden eggs?

The prophets of doom will wring their hands and wail that investment incentives will be impaired, that capital will flee the country, that all the rich will emigrate to Liechtenstein or the Bahamas, that profits will drop, that production will fall, that the nation's economic growth will be impaired, that the economy will be destroyed, that we will bust the bungs out of the barrel, that the stock market will collapse permanently, that grass will grow in the streets, and that the country will suffer a depression to end all depressions.

Dire predictions that never came about also accompanied the introduction of income and inheritance taxes. The Official Investment Bankers Association warned, "This is the beginning of the death of capitalism." Congressman Joseph C. Hendrix of New York denounced the income tax as one that "punished enterprise and drives capital into idleness and hiding." Seth L. Millikan of Maine called it a "penalty upon the industry, frugality, temperate habits, enterprise and persistent effort by which great fortunes are achieved." Thaddeus Stevens had termed the progressive income tax "a punishment of the rich man because he is rich."

Back in Roman times, Pliny the Younger denounced the death tax as "an unnatural tax, augmenting the sorrow of the bereaved." Senator Williams V. Allen of Nebraska ridiculed the tax collectors who "stand with the widow and children at the graveside of a dead father to collect a tax."

The income tax and the inheritance tax have been in effect for decades. The nation has prospered by leaps and bounds during this period. Neither persons nor capital have fled the country. Where could they run: Costa Rica? No one discerns long lines of persons relinquishing their United States citizenship. Investment has not suffered.

It is argued that if the more a man earns, the more he is taxed, then it will not be worthwhile for him to aim at increasing his income. Rational claims for income and wealth inequality boil down to the need for incentives: that American capitalism will come to an end should these privileges be curtailed, or that economic growth will grind to a halt if incentives are tampered with.

In the United States, however, the growth of economic production has been substantially greater since World War II, although the tax burden has been much greater. The same pattern is true in other advanced industrial countries.

A study by Thomas Sanders entitled *Effects of Taxation on Executives* concluded that effort is not significantly reduced by high taxation. How many people do you know who, given the choice between fame and fortune, will not choose fame? For a bit of ribbon, men have over and over again throughout the ages, performed services no money could have brought.

And what of the poor? What incentive would they have under a negative income tax? Would they stop working if they were promised a guaranteed minimum income?

We had previously mentioned the Goodwin and Ferman-Miller studies. A recent three-year project conducted by the Institute for Research on Poverty at the University of Wisconsin, under the direction of Harold Watts, reported the exact opposite. They found that poor people kept working even when they knew that they could receive the same income if they quit their jobs. The researchers studied the economic and psychological impact of weekly income supplements on the lives of 725 poor families in five cities in New Jersey and Pennsylvania, and 450 families in rural areas of Iowa and North Carolina.

The families were guaranteed an annual income of either fifty percent, seventy-five percent, one hundred percent, or 125 percent of the poverty line, which was about $4,275 for a family of four when the study began. As a further variable, each family was subject to a tax rate on its earned income of either thirty, fifty, or seventy percent. The result was that each family faced a break-even point, at which it earned no more by working than it could by relying totally on the income supplement.

Professor Watts summed up, "Anyone who expected the people to stop working, sit on their front porch and whittle is in for a surprise."

Clearly the processes of growth are much more complex than the incentive argument would suggest. This argument cloaks self-interest in the guise of general welfare and is usually warped into a rationalization for the status quo.

Let us turn now to the familiar claim that a net-worth levy would destroy capital investment and economic growth. A similar argument is made that equalizing the capital-gain tax would impair investment incentives. But these arguments just do not hold water.

For example, the rise in the alternative capital-gain tax from twenty-five percent to thirty-five percent in the 1969 Tax Reform Act did not have the effect of reducing investment.

Further, we must recognize that the great bulk of investment in new plant and equipment is financed by corporations—not individuals—out of retained earnings and depreciation allowances. Butters, Thompson, and Bollinger, in *Effects of Taxation: Investment by Individuals,* conclude that the role of the individual investor as a source of venture capital is "grossly exaggerated." Adolf Berle in *Power Without Property* also concluded that "only a tiny fragment of risk capital is ventured by individuals."

The balance of investment capital is now provided, in the main, by institutions, such as pension funds, endowment funds, insurance companies, labor unions, universities, and the like. They will continue to invest in American industry, even with a wealth tax because investment is their *raison d'etre.* If they stopped investing, what would they do with their funds?

We have dealt with the negative arguments against a new tax program for America. For reasons we have previously outlined, it is too dangerous to maintain that nothing can be done to make the tax system more equitable and more productive.

What are the positive arguments for a new tax program for America?

1. Technically sound.
2. Fair and equitable.

It is comprehensive tax reform meeting the two tests of equity:

1. Horizontal equity through equal taxation of all measures of ability to pay, regardless of source.
2. Vertical equity through progressivity.

The program is based on the three measures of ability to pay: receipts, expenditures, and wealth. Since it is levied directly on individuals, corporations, and similar entities it is capable of being levied with the graduation and differentiation of rates that is necessary for an equitable tax structure. The burden cannot be shifted easily onto the shoulders of the masses.

The program is a better-balanced tax system than one concentrating on income alone. A tendency for the wealth tax to cut down the rate of capital accumulation and encourage purchasing nondurable rather than durable goods would be countered by the expenditures tax. A combination of the two taxes—expenditure and wealth—however, far from cancelling the good effects of either, make it possible to restrict effectively the living standards of the rich without sacrificing the long-run egalitarian objective of a more even distribution of property. There is no question but that a progressive expenditures tax would do far more than the present system of income taxation to equalize the standard of living of the different classes, thereby bringing us nearer to social and economic equality.

The program offers far fewer potential dangers to economic development. On the contrary, it would encourage the growth of industry. Given sufficient wealth, what is to stop the rich man from hoarding cash? But when this barren cash bears a net-worth tax like any other asset, then there would be a strong incentive to push towards equity capital instead. A progressive system of taxation will encourage capital accumulations by those who do not yet have much wealth. Since the net-worth tax would be levied only on nonhuman capital, the tendency would be to invest more in education.

At present, it is sad to see so much useful energy consumed in tax avoidance and evasion, to see the huge inventiveness of the accounting profession deflected into a task that in the end produces little to enrich society. Our tax program is simple to administer. It is self-auditing. It will not require an army of bureaucrats. It will eliminate the need for a horde of tax lawyers, tax shelter peddlers, lobbyists, and special interest pleaders.

It is the growing conviction of a great number of laboring people and others that the American tax system today is grossly unfair; it bears down too heavily on lower and middle-income people whose earnings come entirely or largely from wages and salaries. They know that the costs of government are not being shared fairly. The people are beginning to see through the public relations trick of falsely identifying the interests of ordinary individuals with those of the wealthy. To paraphrase President Nixon, it is natural for a worker to resent seeing a large chunk of his hard-earned wage taken by government to give to someone else who may refuse to work—even if that someone else happens to be rich. The obvious unfairness and inequities of our tax structure are major reasons for the disaffection that is abroad in our land. This is what breeds cynicism and erodes confidence in our government.

Perhaps these inequities might be justified if one could show that they encouraged industry and solid production of goods and services. But no, the emphasis of the tax law has shifted, in the main, towards favoring the promoter, the fast buck shill, the manipulator, the get-rich-quick artist, the conniver, the conglomerate builder, the speculator. These new captains of finance never go near a factory and could not care less about production. They wax rich not by supplying the public, but by shuffling pieces of paper. They typically become enriched not by industry, but by finance, not by management, but by promotion and speculation. The richest rewards go to the closest students of the tax laws.

The American tax system has been, and is, an agency of antisocial priorities. It should be turned upside down.

The tax laws are encouraging a system about which Maynard Keynes wrote,

> Speculation may do no more harm than a tar bubble on a steady stream of enterprise. But the position is serious when enterprise becomes the bubble on a whirlpool of speculation. When the capital development of a country becomes the by-product of the activities of a casino, the job is likely to be ill-done.

Our tax structure has drifted far afield from the American standard of fair play. Thomas Jefferson expressed that standard as "equal rights to all; special privileges to none." To a considerable extent, American social policy has developed out of the belief that each generation of individuals should stand on its own with a minimum of handicapping by previous generations.

Andrew Carnegie expressed this belief,

> Why should men leave great fortunes to their children? If this is done from affection, is it most misguided affection? . . . Observation teaches that, generally speaking, it is not well for the children that they should be so burdened . . . . The thoughtful man would as soon leave to his sons a curse as the almighty dollar.

Mr. Carnegie, therefore, believed the estate tax to be the "wisest" levy. It saved the children of the wealthy from the temptation of leading "a less useful and less worthy life."

The proposed tax program is not a soak-the-rich panacea. Given the sources of revenue available, the tax rates should be on the modest size, even in the highest brackets. It is not intended to solve the ills of America overnight in one fell swoop, by levying confiscatory taxes on the well-to-do. Rather, what is intended is a gradual whittling down of those inequities that fuel the American pressure cooker.

Theoretically, a just system of taxation distributes the burden of taxation in accordance with the benefits conferred by the State. The expenses of government are largely caused by the protection of property. John Locke stated, "Government has no other end than the preservation of property."

It is only right that those most able to afford the cost and having the most interest in the preservation of a stable government should contribute their full share of the funds requisite to maintain and uphold that government.

The proposed tax program taxes nobody but those who can pay. It brings the least distress to any living being because it taxes the surpluses and not the necessities. It is a tax on wealth and not on want. President Andrew Johnson, a century ago, set forth the principle that "taxes should be so distributed as not to fall unduly on the poor, but rather on the accumulated wealth of the country."

There is widespread agreement in principle in the United

States on the need to redistribute some income and wealth from the rich to the poor to the end that the less fortunate should be provided for as a matter of right in a just society. It is really part and parcel of the American boast and dream of equal opportunity. Yet, equality of opportunity is, and will remain, in part, a mirage until large concentrations of wealth are broken up. The passing on from generation to generation of large inheritances is the antithesis of equal opportunity.

While the notion of equality of opportunity does not imply that income and wealth should be distributed equally, extreme concentrations represent an insurmountable barrier to those below and a permanent crutch for those above. The proposed tax program would act as a brake against further extreme concentrations.

It is the belief of this writer that a substantial proportion of the rich and well-born would gladly relinquish this permanent crutch. Witness the large number of flower children who deserted the comforts and amenities of home. No one, not even the rich, wants to be the object of public welfare. Given the choice, the probability is that the rich, as well as the poor, would reject the welfare ethic in favor of the work ethic. The rich do not wish to be exempt from some striving and some sacrifice. Yes, Mr. Nixon, "self-reliance and willingness to work make a person—even a rich person—a better human being."

This writer agrees with George McGovern "that even those who are rich and well born would feel happier if they paid their fair share of the cost of making this the great land it should be."

No single step would do more to restore the faith of the American people in the integrity and impartiality of their government and their institutions than the passage of a system of equitable taxation. A reasonable tax reform program is possible. It deserves a high place on the national agenda. This writer submits that his tax program tenders such a reasonable system to the American people. He offers it for their consideration.

16

A Plea

Permit me to close as I began, with a plea to the one percent of the population who owns America to whom this book is addressed.

Pay heed to the discontent that is rampant in our land. Pay heed to the cries of the hungry, the ill, the dispossessed, the disadvantaged. The riots in the cities have subsided. No one knows when they will flare up again. The campus unrest has subsided. No one knows when it will burst forth again, exploding like the boiler of a steam engine. The 1968 Paris-uprising caught General De Gaulle by surprise. Two years before the Russian Revolution, Lenin stated that although a socialist revolution was sure to come, his generation would not live to see it. Proudhon wrote that the fecundity of the unexpected far exceeds the prescience of the statesman.

We had earlier listed the prerequisites of revolution that are present in full force in the present-day United States. The Rev. Dr. Martin Luther King, Jr. voiced the most eloquent expression of this discontent in an address to students at Oslo University,

> The deep rumbling of discontent that we hear today is the thunder of disinherited masses rising from dungeons of oppression to the

bright hills of freedom, in one majestic chorus the rising masses are singing, in the words of our freedom song, "Ain't Gonna Let Nobody Turn Us Around."

We all hear and feel the inner rumbling of the volcano. It can continue to rumble indefinitely. Or it can erupt at any moment. The answer depends on whether a spark—perhaps a severe economic downturn—happens to ignite the tinderbox. The answer depends on whether a leader—undoubtedly he will be a magnetic demagogue, a spellbinding gangster—who is able to voice and focus the resentment and frustration of the people happens to arise to light the way for the masses.

An ancient Chinese proverb states, "To prophesy is extremely difficult especially with respect to the future." In any event, it makes little sense to sit in the mouth of the volcano, wring one's hands, bemoan one's fate, and do nothing. General Omar N. Bradley warned, "We can't sit about waiting for some felicitous accident of history that may somehow make the world all right. Time is running against us." The least one can do is buy volcano insurance. It is up to the wealthy one percent to come forward to silence the discontent.

While the cities are not on fire at the moment of this writing, most of the conditions that caused the civil disorders in recent years have worsened. It is only that the direction of struggle has temporarily taken a new turn towards the populism we discussed earlier. What the new populism portends is an update of Marxist class struggle, the prize being the political power to penalize and punish one group for the benefit of another. Big business, if not all business, is the clear target of the new populism, the central plank of whose platform is "blast the rich."

After all, thirty million people did vote for George McGovern, and that fact should convey some sort of message. The Democratic position on privilege had been made perfectly clear. To quote Mr. McGovern, "The federal tax system . . . has been riddled with special privileges for the rich. We should move now to establish a fair tax system for all

Americans." Another voice of the majority party, Hubert Humphrey had declared, "The time has come for a tax system that says to the wealthy, to the superrich, to big busines, to the bankers, 'You must pay your fair share.' " A third important voice, Edmund Muskie, added,

> Unless we win sweeping tax reform, we will propose our programs and speak about our solutions and enact laws and we will still find social and economic justice beyond our grasp. We must change our tax system so we can change this country without telling poor and middle-class Americans to sacrifice beyond their means.

Jimmy Carter and Walter Mondale are in that populist tradition.

True, Mr. Nixon and the Republican party won the 1972 Presidental election by an overwhelming vote. Julian Bond explained that victory as the

> movement of the comfortable, the callous and the smug closing their ranks and their hearts against the claims and calls to conscience put forward by the forgotten and unrepresented elements in American society.

By itself, however, the size of the vote is not decisive, especially if we take into account that only 54.5 percent of those eligible bothered to vote. The lists did not, thanks to Senator Sam Ervin and the Watergate Committee, close forever after 1972. The 1976 election righted the balance.

Societies do not knit together or come apart by majority vote. What is more important, according to Barrington Moore, Jr., is the intensity of disbelief, the willingness to put your body on the line for your beliefs and the location of disbelievers in the social system.

On this score, it is reasonably plain that a very significant element among those normally expected to run America within the next ten years now bitterly rejects everything America signifies. The same is true, though for very different reasons, of an equally significant element of those normally expected to remain patiently and uncomplainingly at the bottom of the social and economic heap. The bitterness is sufficiently deep and located in sufficiently strategic parts of the social structure to cause nightmares to the powers that be.

When Mr. Barr warned Congress in 1969 of the possibility of a taxpayer revolt led by the middle classes "if we do not soon make major reforms in our income taxes," he stated that the system depends on widespread confidence that it is fair "and that everyone is paying according to his ability to pay." Since that date, a growing body of the electorate has become angrily aware of the favoritism of the tax laws. Public opinion polls offer fairly clear evidence that a majority of Americans think that the rich get away with murder on taxation.

A poll conducted by the Opinion Research Corporation in 1971 found that only sixteen percent of those interviewed felt that taxes should be as high as they are, while only twenty-three percent felt that they were getting their money's worth. A similar poll conducted by Louis Harris in the same year found that sixty-nine percent of the public sympathized with a tax revolt—up from forty-three percent in 1969. A 1972 poll by this organization showed that seventy-one percent of all Americans want taxes raised for the rich and lowered for the middle and low-income people. In 1956 the corresponding percentage was twenty-two percent. The 1972 Harris survey indicated that at least two out of every three persons in the United States believed that the tax laws are written for the rich.

One begins to understand why George Wallace, Mr. McGovern, Mr. Humphrey, Mr. Muskie and Mr. Carter pitched so major a portion of their 1972 and 1976 campaigns towards the issue of taxes. Americans are up in arms over taxes. Tax reform has become the test, the touchstone, the key towards social and economic justice in the United States. A political leader who does not come out unequivocably for tax reform fails the litmus test of his willingness to correct the ills that are undermining America.

The then Mayor John Lindsay stated, "What some one ought to do is to organize a nationwide grass roots campaign for a total tax restructuring in this country by 1976, the bicentennial. Whoever does will have a great political future." Mr. Carter did just that.

An idea, such as tax reform, directed towards a more equitable America, cannot be muted indefinitely. Victor Hugo wrote, "More powerful than armies is an idea whose time has come." The normal processes of law—including tax laws—are sufficient only when the majority of people to whom they apply accept these laws and, in fact, approve of them. Since this is manifestly not the case as far as the tax laws are concerned, it is only a matter of time before these laws, which go directly to the heart of American life, must change—peaceably or otherwise.

Wilbur Mills stated, as far back as 1958, "We can no longer afford to defer serious, large scale efforts to revise our federal tax system." Congressman Charles A. Vanik, Democrat of Ohio, in October 1973, mentioned the existence of "what I see as a crying demand from the American people for tax reform."

The way in which a society shares the fruits of its land and resources is the most fundamental of all the determinations that it must make; especially is this so in a democracy. Redistribution is in the air in America today. This should not be surprising. The equitable distribution of wealth and income has always been accepted as an unalterable given of American democracy.

Congressman Henry S. Reuss stated,

> I believe that there is no defect of democracy which more democracy can't cure. I think the country prospers best when the distribution of wealth and income is not too unequal, when power is decentralized, when institutions—government, business, unions,—are of a size and not so big that they lose human scale.

The Homestead Act of 1862 was such a wealth distribution measure. The Sixteenth Amendment was designed to achieve similar results. Thomas Jefferson stated, "Legislators cannot invent too many devices for subdividing property." These are political and social objectives. From the economic sector, Leon Keyserling tells us that equitable distribution is a prerequisite for stable growth.

Louis Kelso and others have proposed various schemes for a redistribution of wealth—otherwise than by socialism or communism—through share the wealth or people's capitalism programs with some sort of reasonable limit on the accumulation of wealth in one's lifetime.

There are other less-delicate methods of wealth redistribution. Burglaries, robberies, and muggings are, at least in part, means of wealth redistribution to which the poor resort when society pays no attention to their expectations. John A. Hamilton, in an article entitled *The Great Drug Rip-Off,* described an interview with a "bulky black woman" who directed a large New York City financed drug treatment program on Saint Ann's Avenue in the slums of the South Bronx. "We have a drug program that serves the people," she said, "If you don't serve the people up here in the Bronx, they will come down to expensive neighborhoods like Greenwich Village and murder you in your bedroom." Psychologists explain that crime is a lashing out against society in unfocused rage through the pathologies associated with poverty and powerlessness.

Since it would be patently unworkable, economically and politically, to return to the small number of capital owners all the fruits of their capital, the scales are also readjusted, more delicately, in a variety of other ways—feather bedding, welfare, charity, full employment, tolerated unionism, high wages, etc.

There is a much more efficacious method of wealth redistribution—a wealth tax. This writer maintains that the most effective, most equitable, and most painless form of wealth redistribution lies within the tax structure. Next to crime, tax policy is probably the quickest device for altering wealth and income distribution.

It lies within the power of our top one percent to utilize this mechanism voluntarily to forestall much more drastic action initiated by others. Further, a wealth tax is the best demonstration of the dedication of the top one percent to the principles of democracy. Call it participatory democracy, if you will. For the issue of tax inequality has stirred a national debate unequalled since the days of William Jennings Bryan.

If we look back in American history, we find that great grass roots mass movements spring up to grapple with the great issues of the past such as slavery, women's suffrage, prohibition and world peace.

The number of mass organizations formed recently to grapple with the issue of taxes is testimony to the overriding importance which that issue has assumed for American society. We might mention the Tax Action Campaign of Fred R. Harris, the Urban Coalition of John Gardner, the Tax Reform Research Group of Ralph Nader, Taxation with Representation of Thomas F. Field, the Boston Tax Action Coalition, New York Citizens for Tax Reform, and the Taxpayers' Rights Association for Houston among others. Tax lawyers are forming public-interest law firms, such as Tax Analysts and Advocates, to represent the public at large against the special pleaders. Citizen Action groups are forming in Chicago and elsewhere.

The influence of the groups arrayed against a significant redistribution of the tax burden is enormous and, until very recently, there was no effective lobby for the poor and the near poor. Former Senator Harris of Oklahoma, recalling his own days on the Senate's tax-writing Finance Committee, said in an interview, "I never heard from anybody but the oil companies . . . What we didn't have was people outside the door."

The people are now outside the door. Will the top one percent welcome them in? It is the purpose of this chapter to show that such an invitation is in the best interest of the top one percent.

Anatole France stated, "Whoso is possessed of the world's goods fears the evil effects of any change." Admittedly, it is difficult to convince the man holding four aces to ask for a new deal. But when the choice is between a new deal and a new deck, the answer becomes clear. If change is not in the interest of the establishment neither is social disorder, since the establishment has the most to lose. The American system is rich enough to buy social peace through help to the underprivileged.

The virtue of the American political system has been its ability to assimilate social transformations without the dissenters having to overthrow the Constitution violently or, generally speaking, the rules.

Ellmore C. Patterson, Chairman of the Board of Morgan Guaranty Trust Company, said in a speech to the American Club in Paris in April 1972 that business owed a vote of thanks to its critics. He noted that businessmen, while not instinctively activists or social reformers, do respond to pressure since their talent is in solving problems. Time and again, business has coopted its critics by adopting their causes, thereby nullifying their slogans.

Thus, Edward B. Rust, the president of the Chamber of Commerce of the United States recognized that Ralph Nader was miscast as an "enemy" of the American business system. Instead, Mr. Nader is committed to making the free-enterprise system work as it is supposed to work—to make market-place realities of the very virtues businessmen ascribe to the system. (The Chamber promptly published a disclaimer.). Gerald M. Loeb, long one of the most influential men on Wall Street and the author of *The Battle for Investment Survival,* declared that, "investor belief in corporate integrity must be restored if our capitalist system is to survive."

Businessmen are pragmatists. With their daily feedback from the market place, they are ready to abandon dogma whenever their survival instinct alerts them to existing realities.

Thus, David Rockefeller, chairman of the Chase Manhattan Bank, urged businessmen to become reformers themselves, making a conscious effort to adapt the market system to our changing social, political, and technological environment. He writes,

> It is up to businessmen to make common cause with other reformers—whether in Government or on the campus or wherever—to prevent the unwise adoption of extreme and emotional remedies, but on the contrary to initiate necessary reforms that will make it possible for business to continue to function in a new climate as a constructive force in our society.

Ralph Nader, speaking as a consumer advocate, remarked,

> The corporate system has a greater absorptive capacity than Mandarin China and more resilience than the Vatican. Corporations, yielding when they were forced to, have in the end overwhelmed populism, organized labor, the New Deal, the regulatory state and they will so overwhelm the consumer movement.

In the 1972 campaign, sixty millionaires took a pledge to finance only those candidates who were committed to reforming the very system that made them candidates. That is the tradition that has enabled the Democratic party to become the longest-lived political party in the world. It has lasted longer than any other party in any country because it has recurrently welcomed and absorbed the emerging ideas in American life.

A society can always attempt to solve its problems by repression or by ignoring them so that it fails to take even the most obvious steps to avert trouble. But solving problems by rigidity or repression instead of trying to cope with them produces a tense and claustrophobic society. Such methods are contradictory to the genius of America that has consistently blunted and embraced unhappy groups, defusing dissent by embodying their grievances into the American mainstream.

Thus, we have affirmed Social Security, the minimum wage, full employment, the United Nations, medicare, public housing, disarmament, and clean air as integral parts of the American scene.

Once having acknowledged the need to bring social justice to America principally through the redistribution of income and wealth, it will not be necessary to move hastily to expropriation or other extremist actions. We are proposing a five to ten-year transition period and limited redistribution. Adoption of the principle of redistribution coupled with the establishment of a definite timetable should by itself calm the fires of discontent.

There is a tendency to under-rate the resiliency of the American economy. But given the cushion of time, there should be no trouble in absorbing the negative income tax and a wealth tax. Yet, it will take time to work out the mechanics of a wealth tax. As Thomas Jefferson said,

> The ground of liberty is to be gained by inches; we must be contented to secure what we can get, from time to time, and eternally press forward for what is yet to get. It takes time to persaude men to do even what is for their own good.

Alfred North Whitehead, one of the foremost philosophers of this century, said shortly before he died, "The art of progress is to preserve order amid change, and to preserve change amid order."

Although recognizing that inequity is endemic to human societies, the first step is to solemnly acknowledge that every decent society must define a floor below which none of its members will be permitted to fall. There are limits to the contrasts of poverty and affluence that people will tolerate when they believe the credo of a society that proclaims that all men are equal and that none is prescribed by birth to low stations or high. Today there is reason to believe that the United States has transgressed those limits.

The years since World War II have witnessed a rise in the expectations of the poor and of the middle-class Americans who are beginning to demand a larger share of the national pie of wealth and power. This is hardly a sign of decline or decadence but rather of vitality and a will to improve.

Robert J. Lampman states, "We could have an efficient capitalist system with far less inequity." Presumably, since wealth is a good thing to have, it would be good for all families to have some. Also, it would seem that the wider the distribution of wealth, the broader the political base of capitalism.

True, it is to the best interests of the top one percent to defuse dissent, to increase the gross national product, to open new markets, to train new workers. Yet, this is not just a matter of self-interest or necessity. Above all, it is a matter of moral right. The philosopher David Hume believed that "fellow feeling with others" is the main force binding men together with society, and the basic foundation of human morals and culture.

The powers that be must recognize that the main business of government is not just to keep order and encourage commerce. The establishment of justice is also the business of government. In the words of Justice William O. Douglas, "For the Republic to survive we must practice charity."

How can the top one percent—or any of us—rest easy when we know that there are, today, children who are without food, thousands who are ill and without adequate care, older men and women who are without hope, and workers who toil for inadequate reward. Is there no sense of fierce outrage at social injustice gnawing at our gut?

Have we as a people lost our capacity to respond? Are we Americans or are we demoralized Ik of northern Uganda who oblige our children to fend for themselves at the age of three, who abuse and starve our elders or leave them indifferently to die, and whose every hand is raised against our neighbor's?

We stand accused of that Biblical indictment:

> For I was hungry and ye gave me no meat; I was thirsty and ye gave me no drink; I was a stranger and ye took me not in; naked and ye clothed me not; sick and ye visiteth me not; a prisoner and ye came not to see me.

The greatest failing of our times is the lack of compassion so that men have become indifferent to the sufferings of millions. Willy Brandt, at a party convention, made an appeal for "compassion," urging, "Have the courage to show this kind of sympathy. Have the courage to be merciful. Have the courage to attend to your neighbor. Recall these so oft-buried values. Find your way back to yourselves."

Human life has become more devaluated than the dollar. We have lost our natural sympathy for our less fortunate brothers. Jean Jacques Rousseau wrote two hundred years ago that there was "an innate repugnance at seeing a fellow creature suffer." Have we become more calloused in the past two hundred years?

More particularly, we have witnessed, since the turn of the century, a period of moral debasement during which a pall of dull acceptance has settled over the American soul, accompanied by deadening of sensibility, a privatization of life, a tendency on the part of each citizen of substance to retreat to the cultivation of his own suburban garden. Gunnar Myrdal, the Swedish economist, reports, "America, of all the rich countries, is the one which has the highest rate of unemployment, the worst and biggest slums, and which is least generous in giving economic security to its old people, its sick and its invalids."

Perhaps it is our vast, impersonal cities that account for such cold detachment from what is happening to a fellow creature in one's immediate vicinity. Gabriel Marcel and others have made perceptive and disturbing analyses of the various modes of degradation, dehumanization, and depersonalization to which we have been subjected during the twentieth century. Modern techniques have enabled us to look at ourselves and our fellowmen abstractly and statistically as mere units, parts and functions, and to become appendages rather than controllers of our machine civilization.

The new technology—coupled with our unending wars—has metamorphized Americans into moral eunuchs, deformed moral cripples, afflicted with moral paralysis. We are a people so weary of hunger and deprivation and death that we have been drained of emotional response. A few hundred thousand more Asians killed at a distance; a few hundred thousand more American children hungry on the other side of the railroad tracks; a few hundred thousand more Americans teetering on the brink of animal subsistence in our teeming ghettos: what has that to do with the rest of us?

Woe unto you that are rich! Unto you that are full!

Heed the plea of Mark, "Have pity on this multitude." Paul's First Epistle to the Corinthians tells us, "And though I have the gift of prophecy and understand all mysteries and all knowledge, and though I have faith so that I could remove mountains, and have not charity, I am nothing." Faith, hope, and charity—the greatest of all these is charity. Yes, there is nothing like charity to take the stink out of a rich man.

At a special assembly of the United Nations Food and Agriculture Organization, convened in March 1963 to enlist "the conscience of the world" in a crusade against hunger, Pope John XXIII of blessed memory declared that it was the immediate duty of society "to bring concrete assistance to those of its members who are deprived of the minimum essential to the normal flowering of their personality."

His enclyclical *Pacem in Terris* spelled out this minimum essential:

> every man has the right to life, to bodily integrity and to the means which are necessary and suitable for the proper development of life. These are primarily food, clothing, shelter, rest, medical care and, finally, the necessary social services. Therefore, a human being also has the right to security in cases of sickness, inability to work, widowhood, old age, unemployment, or in any other case in which he is deprived of the means of subsistence through no fault of his own.

Pope Paul VI, in an address marking the church's annual Day of Peace, 1 January 1972, added, "The littler, the poorer, the more defenseless, even the lower a man has fallen, the more he deserves to be assisted, raised up, cared for and honored. We learn this from the Gospel."

Heed the commandment of Jesus to his apostles, "Heal the sick, cleanse the lepers, raise the dead, cast out devils: freely ye have received, freely give."

Freely ye have received, freely give. "Take my yoke upon you, and learn from me; for I am meek and lowly in heart: and ye shall find rest unto your souls."

Who knows? Charity may even be profitable. For instance, ten years ago, the gross national product of the black community was estimated at less than twenty billion dollars. Today it is said to be more than fifty billion dollars. Properly nurtured, it can go to one hundred billion dollars.

We must recognize that the welfare of each is the welfare of all. Eugene V. Debs wrote in *Walls and Bars:*

> While there is a lower class I am in it,
> While there is a criminal element I am of it;
> While there is a soul in prison I am not free.

For the nation that engineered the lift to the moon, the challenge is to wed its resources with its compassion to build a humane community—a community that does not deaden awareness and brutalize feeling, but that is sensitized to the dire need of eradicating poverty—the cancer that is eating away at all our citizenry.

Robert Ardrey points out that experiences of fire, flood, and sudden storm, of natural emergencies produce, as if by spontaneous combustion, instant mutual aid, unthinking sacrifice, smiles on the faces of strangers, intimacies exchanged that have never changed hands before—a gladness and trust that leaves us sorry when the emergency has passed. All species lead lives of certain hazard but if you compare species with species, you will discover that as hazard goes up, mechanisms for enmity come down.

This is a period of great emergency and hazard for America. The revolution of rising expectations is accompanied by the revolution of rising resentment on behalf of the newly clamorous masses. What will be the reaction of the top one percent? Will they meet the emergency with aid and sacrifice and gladness and trust?

For the moment, the fate of the poor hangs upon the decision of the better-off. For the moment, we cannot effect redistribution of wealth and income without the goodwill and the cooperation of the better-off. Reverend Skinner tells us that "There's no way you can deal with the oppressed without dealing with the oppressor."

David Rockefeller agrees that, "Some adjustments in the social contract, binding business to society, are inevitable. There may have to be new laws to force consideration of the quality-of-life dimension so that more socially responsive firms will not suffer a competitive disadvantage." Mr. Rockefeller foresees that investment-projects not sufficiently high on the "social agenda" may have to wait in line for approval. Because of the growing pressure for greater corporate responsibility, corporations may be required to publish a "social audit" certified by independent accountants.

Mr. Rockefeller poses the issue: "The question really comes down to this: Will business leaders seize the initiative to make necessary changes and take on new responsibilities voluntarily, or will they wait until these are thrust upon them by law?"

We take the liberty of adding: or thrust upon them by revolution.

A situation so full of bitterness, like of today's United States, can only end in tragedy. Despite the demonstrated genius of America to assimilate dissenting groups, we know that the processes of reform are painfully slow. One has grave misgivings about the sincerity of the efforts of the Establishment's beneficiaries to abandon their game of greed and bring about a peaceable "greening of America." Like privileged groups everywhere, they are slow to yield their august posture. And if the privileged groups, as typified by the Nixon and Ford administrations, continue to make our institutions more rigid and regressive, our internal divisions will certainly deepen.

Jean-Francois Revel poses what he calls the "only question": Will the American political system, the American Constitution, manage to mint a new society or will they be blown up by the endless American crisis? America has no choice today between instituting the basic changes necessary for a just society and witnessing the complete disintegration of that society—and the absence of choice is more or less the definition that M. Revel gives of a "revolutionary system." Since problems have to be solved in one way or another, a failure to resolve them peaceably will cause violence to spread throughout the country to the disruption of the American system.

Violent revolutions have always been substitutes for pacific ones. John F. Kennedy said, "Those who make peaceful revolution impossible will make violent revolution inevitable." The French philosopher Paul Ricoeur reminds us that, "History is violence" and that violence is "the privileged mode in accordance with which the form of history changes."

We have detailed earlier why it is predictable that the coming revolution in America will be violent. We have identified the elements in our society who have, because of alienation from America, become bands of outlaws prepared for guerrilla warfare. Jean Paul Sartre, in his introduction to Fanon's book, states, "it is through mad fury that the wretched of the earth can become men."

The Black Panther Party, in a message to America, delivered on the 107th anniversary of the Emancipation Proclamation at Washington D.C., "capitol of Babylon," on 19 June 1970, calling attention to its "strategic ability to lay this country in ruin from the bottom to the top," declared,

> Forced to respond with a form of War of Salvation that in the chaos of carrying it out and the attempt to repress it will gut this country and utterly destroy it. Before we accept genocide we will inflict Total Destruction upon Babylon.

Former Vice-President Agnew warned that, "People cannot live in a state of perpetual electric shock. Tired of a convulsive society, they settle for an authoritarian society." Riots lead to repression and violence to counterviolence. If there is anarchy, and if it is allowed to spread and grow, at the end there is nothing left but the police state. A nationwide poll conducted by CBS News in 1970 concluded that a majority of American adults are willing to choose order at the expense of some of their liberties.

Secretary of State Henry A. Kissinger stated,

> It has been our conviction that if political decisions were to be made in the streets, the victors would not be upper middle class college kids, but some real tough guys. We have seen examples of that in New York City, and elsewhere, of what happens when this trend develops, and the society which makes its decisions in this manner will sooner or later be driven towards some form of Caesarism in which the most brutal forces in the society will take over. The very people who shout, "Power to the people" are not going to be the people who take over this country if it turns into a test of strength.

In the chaotic months of 1917 preceding the October Revolution in Russia, while the Menshevik wing of the Social Democratic party and Social Revolutionaries toppled the monarchy and struggled for power, violence spread throughout Russia thus permitting the Bolsheviks to seize power.

Witness Chile.

The notion that destruction and chaos will miraculously produce Utopia is refuted by all history. Chairman Mao warns our romantic revolutionary and our top one percent alike,

> A revolution is not a dinner party, or writing an essay, or painting a picture, or doing embroidery; it cannot be so refined, so leisurely and gentle, so temperate, kind, courteous, restrained and magnanimous. A revolution is an insurrection, an act of violence by which one class overthrows another.

Raymond F. Dasmann wrote in the *Lost Horizon*, "It is far easier to overthrow a government than to repair a land." Our militants should not imagine that, if our present system is demolished, they will necessarily inherit the wreckage. History tells us that, all too often, dictators and tyrants pick up the pieces.

We remarked earlier that the charismatic leader who will arise to "light the way" for the masses will undoubtedly be a gangster. "In times of revolution, power will always go to the worst scoundrel," said Danton. A mass movement, particularly in its active, revivalist phase appeals to the failures, the misfits, the outcasts, the criminals, and all those who have lost their footing, or never had one, in the ranks of humanity. In the end, the rulers will emerge from the most aggressive, the most cynical, the most unscrupulous sort of men.

There is no way we can deal with the oppressed without dealing with the oppressor. By the same token, there is no way we can deal with the oppressor without dealing with the oppressed. A plea addressed to the oppressor, to the top one percent who owns America, must, of necessity, embrace the oppressed, the victims, the disaffected.

To the oppressed, we have the duty of pointing out that revolution is decapitation; it usually ends by devouring its own children. Regis Debray, in his famous interview with President Allende of Chile, prophetically asked, "A revolution without terror, is it conceivable?" History does not record a revolution without the execution wall.

Hannah Arendt declares that poverty cannot be eliminated by political upheaval; revolutionary get-rich-quick schemes are bound to founder. In the French Revolution, Robespierre's first efforts were directed towards curing the ills of the masses. When they failed, he turned in rage and frustration to terror, which also did not work. When the terror receded, the hard economic facts remained.

Miss Arendt writes in *On Revolution,*

> We know to our sorrow that freedom has been better preserved in countries where no revolution ever broke out, no matter how outrageous the circumstances of the powers that be, and that there exist more civil liberties even in countries where the revolution was defeated than in those where revolutions have been victorious.

Revolution is an enormously cruel and wasteful way of solving human problems. Thus far in history, the main burden of suffering in these upheavals has fallen upon the masses of little people. Riots make for ruin in the neighborhoods of the poor; disorder destroys the civil liberties of the disadvantaged. Only in order can we build a new society.

In a revolutionary order, we are concerned not with adjustments within a given framework but with the framework itself. It is submitted that the framework of American society is still serviceable. What is required is some adjustments within that framework. One does not throw away a tennis-racket frame that has served the test of time when it only needs restringing.

Nor need the adjustments be extremist or radical. We do not seek a completely rational social order of mathematically precise income and wealth distribution. That is impossible. Nor should such a distant prospect furnish us with grounds for abandoning our efforts to ameliorate the injustices and cruelties that do exist. We seek moderate and modest adjustments to the American framework accomplished over a transitional period of years.

No doubt economic privileges would be swept away in a revolutionary upheaval, but many other things of value in American life—especially culture and civil liberties—would also go up against the egalitarian wall. Surely, the injustices and cruelties and inequalities set forth in this book need to be righted. But let us accomplish our objectives in a careful, selective way—not by a wave of popular malevolence. Although we have reason to be impatient with the painfully slow processes of our democracy, we abandon them at our peril.

It is submitted that the best first step towards building an America based on compassion and social justice is the adoption of a wealth tax. A wealth tax will begin to accomplish the moderate and modest adjustment that we seek for the American framework.

We appeal to the top one percent to give serious consideration to the adoption of a wealth tax. We appeal to the dissidents to be patient long enough to permit the introduction of such a wealth tax. We can think of no other single measure capable, at this moment in our history, of dampening the coals of revolution.

We thus offer America a tax on wealth as an alternative to revolution. Each side ignores this plea at its peril.

"Vengeance is mine; I will repay," saith the Lord.

Bibliography

A selected list of the works consulted or cited:

Books:

Abels, Jules, *The Rockefeller Billions: The Story of the World's Most Stupendous Fortune,* Macmillan, 1965

Ardrey, Robert, *The Social Contract*, Atheneum Publishers, 1970

Arendt, Hannah, *On Revolution*, Viking Press, 1965. *On Violence,* Harcourt Brace Jovanovich, 1970

Baldwin, James, *No Name in the Street,* Dial Press, 1972

Bannock, Graham, *The Juggernauts,* Bobbs-Merrill, 1971

Barlow, Robin et al., *Economic Behavior of the Affluent,* Brookings Institution, 1966

Beard, Charles ., and Mary, R., *The Rise of American Civilization*, Macmillan, 1927

Beard, Marian, *A History of the Business Man,* Macmillan, 1938

Berle, Adolf A., *Power,* Harcourt Brace Jovanovich, 1969. *Power Without Property,* Harcourt Brace Jovanovich, 1959, and Means, Gardiner, C., *The Modern Corporation and Private Property,* Harcourt Brace Jovanovich, 1929

Blackstone, William, *Commentaries on the Laws of England*

Braden, William, *The Age of Aquarius,* Quadrangle, 1970

Brooks, John, *The Go-Go Years,* Weybright and Talley, 1973

Brutus, *Confessions of a Stock Broker*, Little, Brown, 1971

Butters, J. Keith et al., *Effects of Taxation: Investment by Individuals,* Maxwell Publishing, 1953

Cantril, Albert H. and Roll, Charles R., Jr., *Hopes and Fears of the American People,* Potomac Associates, 1971

Carroll, Lewis, *Alice in Wonderland*

Chomsky, Noam, *American Power and the New Mandarins,* Pantheon Press, 1969

Cleaver, Eldridge, *Soul on Ice,* McGraw-Hill, 1969

Commoner, Barry, *The Closing Circle,* Alfred A. Knopf, 1971

Cook, Fred J., *The Corrupted Land,* Macmillan, 1966

Davie, Ronald et al, *From Birth to Seven,* Longman, 1972

Debs, Eugene V., *Walls and Bars,* C.H. Kerr, 1927

Diogenes, *The April Game: Secrets of an Internal Revenue Agent,* Playboy Press, 1973

Domhoff, G. Williams, *Who Rules America,* Prentice-Hall, 1967. *The Higher Circles: The Governing Class in America,* Random House, 1970

DuBois, William E.B., *Black Reconstruction in America,* Atheneum Publishers, 1935

Eisenstein, Louis, *The Ideologies of Taxation,* Ronald Press, 1961

Fanon, Frantz, *Black Skins and White Masks,* Grove Press, 1952 *The Wretched of the Earth,* Grove Press, 1965

Fuchs, Victor, *The Concept of Poverty,* National Bureau of Economic Research, 1965

Galbraith, John K., *The Affluent Society,* Houghton-Mifflin, 1958. *American Capitalism,* Houghton-Mifflin, 1952. *Economics and the Public Purpose,* Houghton-Mifflin, 1973
The Great Crash, Houghton-Mifflin, 1955. *The New Industrial State,* Houghton-Mifflin, 1967

George, Henry, *Progress and Poverty,* Robert Schalkenbach Foundation, 1879

Goldsmith, Raymond W., *A Study of Savings in the United States,* Princeton University Press, 1956

Goodman, Paul, *Growing Up Absurd,* Random House, 1956

Goodwin, Leonard, *Do the Poor Want to Work?* Brookings Institution, 1972

Green, Mark J. et al., *The Closed Enterprise System,* Grossman Publishers, 1972

Hacker, Andrew, *End of the American Era,* Antheneum Publishers, 1971

Harrington, Michael, *The Other America: Poverty in the United States,* Macmillan, 1962. *Socialism,* Saturday Review Press, 1972

Harris, Fred R., *The New Populism,* Saturday Review Press, 1973

Heilbroner, Robert L., *Between Capitalism and Socialism,* Random House, 1970. *In the Name of Profit,* Doubleday, 1972. *The Limits of American Capitalism,* Harper and Row, 1966

Hoffman, Abbie, *Revolution for the Hell of It,* Dial Press, 1968

Holy Bible

Hollings, Ernest F., *The Case Against Hunger,* Cowles Publishing, 1970

Jacoby, Neil H., *Corporate Power and Social Responsibility,* Macmillan, 1975

Jay, Antony, *Machiavelli and Management,* Holt, Rinehart and Winston, 1968

Josephson, Matthew, *The Robber Barons,* Harcourt Brace Jovanovich, 1934

Kaldor, Nicholas, *An Expenditure Tax,* George Allen Publishing, 1955

Kelso, Louis O. and Adler, Mortimer, *The Capitalist Manifesto,* Greenwood Press, 1958, and Hetter, Patricia, *How to Turn Eighty Million Workers into Capitalists on Borrowed Money,* Random House, 1967

Kerstein, George G., *The Rich: Are They Different?,* Houghton-Mifflin, 1968

Keynes, John Maynard, *General Theory of Employment, Interest and Money,* Harcourt Brace Jovanovich, 1934. *How to Pay for the War,* Collected Writings, St. Martin's Press

Kolko, Gabriel, *Wealth and Power in America,* Praeger Publishers, 1962

Kuznetz, Simon, *Shares of Upper Income Groups in Income and Savings,* National Bureau of Economics Research, 1953

Lampman, Robert J., *The Share of the Top Wealth Holders in National Wealth, 1922-1956,* Princeton University Press, 1962

Larson, Martin A., *The Great Tax Fraud,* Devin-Adair Publishing, 1968

Lazarus, Simon, *Genteel Populists,* Holt, Rinehart and Winston, 1974

Loeb, Gerald M., *Battle for Investment Survival,* Simon and Schuster, 1965

Lundberg, Ferdinand, *The Rich and the Super-Rich,* Lyle Stuart, 1968

Malcolm X, *Autobiography,* Ballantine Books, 1973

Mao Tse-tung, *Quotations*

Marx, Karl, *Capital,* Modern Library. *Class Struggles in France,* C.H. Kerr

Miller, Herman, P., *Rich Man, Poor Man,* Thomas Y. Crowell Publishing, 1971

Mills, C. Wright, *The American Political Elite: A Collective Portrait,* Oxford University Press, 1950. *The Power Elite,* Oxford University Press, 1956. *White Collar,* Oxford University Press, 1951

Mintz, Morton and Cohen, Jerry S., *America, Inc.: Who Owns and Operates the United States?* Dial Press, 1971

Mitford, Jessica, *Kind and Unusual Punishment: The Prison Business,* Alfred A. Knopf, 1973

Moore, Barrington, Jr., *Reflections on the Causes of Human Misery and Upon Certain Proposals to Eliminate Them,* Beacon Press, 1970

Moynihan, Daniel P., *The Politics of a Guaranteed Income,* Random House, 1972

Musgrave, Richard A. and Peacock, A.T., *Classics in the Theory of Public Finance,* St. Martin's Press, 1964

Myers, Gustavus, *The Ending of Hereditary American Fortunes,* Julian Messner, 1939. *History of the Great American Fortunes,* C.H. Kerr, 1927

Myrdal, Gunnar, *An American Dilemma: The Negro Problem and Modern Democracy,* Harper and Row, 1962. *Challenge to Affluence,* Patheon Books, 1963

Newfield, Jack and Greenfield, Jeff, *A Populist Manifesto: The Making of a New Majority,* Praeger Publishing, 1972

Newman, Herbert E., *Introduction to Public Finance,* John Wiley Publishing, 1968

Nutter, G. Warren and Einhorn, Henry A., *Enterprise Monopoly in the United States, 1899-1958,* Colorado University Press, 1969

Orwell, George, *1984,* Harcourt Brace Jovanovich, 1949

Osborn, William C., *The Paper Plantation,* Grossman Publishers, 1974

Parker, Richard, *Myth of the Middle Class,* Liveright Publishing, 1972

Paul, Randolph, *Taxation in the United States,* Little, Brown, 1954

Pechman, Joseph A., *The Public Interest,* Brookings Institution and Breale, George F., *Federal Tax Reform: The Impossible Dream?* Brookings Institution, 1975

Piven, Frances Fox and Cloward, Richard A., *Regulating the Poor,* Pantheon Books, 1970

Reich, Charles A., *The Company State,* Random House, 1971. *Greening of America,* Random House, 1970

Reisman, David, *Class in American Society,* Free Press, 1960. *The Lonely Crowd,* Yale University Press, 1950

Revel, Jean-Francois, *Without Marx or Jesus,* Doubleday, 1970

Robinson, James H., *Mind in the Making,* Harper and Row, 1921

Roszak, Theodore, *The Making of a Counter Culture,* Doubleday, 1969, and Betty, *Masculine/Feminine,* Harper and Row, 1921

Ruskay, Joseph A. and Osserman, Richard A., *Halfway to Tax Reform,* Indiana University Press, 1970

Ruskin, John, *Unto this Last,* Everyman Library

Samuelson, Paul A., *Economics: An Introductory Analysis,* Mc-Graw-Hill, 1961

Sanders, Thomas, *Effects of Taxation on Executives,* Maxwell Reprint, 1951

Sartre, Jean Paul, *Orpheé Noir,* Panther House, 1971

Servan-Schreiber, J.J., *The American Challenge,* Atheneum Publishers, 1967

Smith, Adam, *An Inquiry in the Nature and Causes of the Wealth of Nations,* Modern Library, 1776

Smith, Adam, *Supermoney,* Random House, 1972

Stamp, Josiah, *Wealth and Taxable Capacity,* Books for Libraries, 1922

Steffins, Lincoln, *Autobiography,* Harcourt Brace Jovanovich, 1931

Steinbeck, John, *Grapes of Wrath,* Viking Press, 1939

Stern, Philip M., *Great Treasury Raid,* Random House, 1964. *Rape of the Taxpayer,* Random House, 1973

Tait, Alan A., *Taxation of Personal Wealth,* University of Illinois Press, 1967

Tebbel, John, *The Inheritors,* Putnam Publishers, 1962

Toffler, Alvin, *Future Shock,* Random House, 1970

Udall, Stewart L., *The Quiet Crisis,* Holt, Rinehart and Winston, 1963

Upjohn, W.E., *Work in America,* Institute for Employment Research, 1972

Veblen, Thorstein, *Theory of the Leisure Class,* Augustus M. Kelley Publishers, 1899

Wattenberg, Benjamin J., *The Real America,* Doubleday, 1974

Whyte, William H., Jr., *Organization Man,* Simon & Schuster, 1956

Wiseman, Thomas, *The Money Motive,* Random House, 1974

Zilg, Gerard C., *du Pont: Behind the Nylon Curtain,* Prentice-Hall, 1974

PERIODICALS:

Armed Forces Journal
Bankers Magazine
British Tax Review
Business Week
Finance
Fortune
Journal of Taxation
New Republic
New York Times
New York Times Magazine
Public Interest
Saturday Review

Time
Wall Street Journal

RESEARCH STUDIES AND GOVERNMENT PUBLICATIONS:

Bach, George L. and Stephenson, James B., *Inflation and the Redistribution of Wealth*

Brookings Institution, *Setting National Priorities: The 1973 Budget*

Budget of the United States Annual Message

Congressional Record

Economic Reports of the President

Federal Commission on Civil Rights, *The Navajo Nation: An American Colony*

Lewis, Arthur M., *Fortune* surveys of individual wealth

National Children's Bureau, *From Birth to Seven*

Statistical Abstract of the United States

United States Department of Commerce, Annual Survey of Manufacturers.

Index